The Friendly Professional

selected writings

Thurstan Brewin

Edited by
Gareth Rees

Thurstan Brewin, FRCP, FRCR

Foreword

Thurstan would never have suggested this. He has had little to do with it, although he was prepared to provide some co-operation in the later stages. The idea of putting together a selection of his writings was enthusiastically received by everyone with whom it was discussed. It needs no further justification. It was equally enthusiastically supported by Anne Parkin and Lederle Laboratories, whose very generous sponsorship has enabled it to become a reality.

After leaving Rugby School Thurstan joined the Army. He was wounded in North Africa, tragically losing a leg, and was taken prisoner. This episode in his life is the subject of Trish Grove's article, 'Christmas 1941' at the beginning of the book. Thurstan became a medical student at Guy's, qualifying in 1949. After house jobs he did medical and radiotherapy registrar jobs at Guy's and the Westminster respectively and then spent five years at the Ontario Cancer Foundation. He became a consultant at the Institute of Radiotherapy and Oncology in Glasgow in 1961. Thurstan retired in 1987 and was then Medical Director of the Marie Curie Foundation for three years. Since 1993 he has been Chairman of HealthWatch.

Thurstan has experienced the cruelty of cancer at close quarters. His adored wife Doreen died of acute leukaemia at the beginning of 1986. They had created a happy and loving family. Thurstan has five children and, so far, nine grandsons and four granddaughters. He lives on the banks of the Thames at Bray, where he paddles his canoe or plays his piano when he needs a break from his desk.

Thurstan has been a thought-provoking and influential author for some 30 years, as well as an eloquent and entertaining speaker. Some of his early publications described his careful documentation of alcohol intolerance and altered appetite and taste in cancer patients. These findings have aroused little interest, a source of some disappointment and surprise to him.

I am very grateful for the help of Rod Robinson of Eurocommunica Publications and also to the editors and publishers of the journals and books for generously releasing copyright without charge. Any profits from the sale of this volume will be donated to the Marie Curie Foundation.

Gareth Rees
Bristol Oncology Centre
September 1995

The Friendly Professional
selected writings of Thurstan Brewin

© Eurocommunica 1996

First published in 1996

Published by:

Eurocommunica Publications
4 Bersted Mews
Bersted Street
Bognor Regis
West Sussex
PO22 9RR
United Kingdom

ISBN: 1 898763 05 4

Printed and bound in Great Britain by
Biddles Ltd, Guildford and King's Lynn

Contents

Christmas 1941

by Trish Groves

Reprinted from
the British Medical Journal,
1990, Vol 301, pages 1467–1468

On Christmas Eve 1941 Lieutenant Thurstan (Tony) Brewin finally located his regiment in the North African desert south east of Benghazi. The colonel who welcomed him was delighted not only by the accompanying cargo of Christmas puddings and mince pies but also because Brewin's arrival meant that he would no longer be the shortest officer in the 11th Hussars.

Just five weeks later the diminutive Brewin was wounded and captured by German troops. When repatriated by the Red Cross in 1943, via Italian hospitals and a prison camp, he was informed that the War Office was *'terminating his employment because of ill health'*. The formal letter did not even mention that he had been wounded in action, let alone acknowledge that he had lost a leg at just 20.

The Ministry of Information was pleased to employ Brewin, however, as a speaker to improve morale in munitions factories. He could start as soon as a quick identity check had been made. This, explained the man from the ministry, was necessary because the best speaker on the circuit had just been exposed as a lifetime landlubber and his rousing tales of being torpedoed had rather lost their edge.

From the notes that Brewin used for his talks for the ministry and the Red Cross comes this account of being wounded and captured.

"Desert nights can be cold and it seemed even more bitter than usual when we climbed into our three armoured cars just before dawn on Thursday 29 January. As we set off towards the enemy Corporal Nottingham bent down to adjust the piece of cardboard which helped to stop the draught from a hole in the armour plate of the turret. Some weeks previously by a tragic error (all too common in mobile desert warfare) a shell from one of our own tanks had torn through that hole and shattered the legs of a young troop leader who had died soon afterwards.

On the skyline, five or six miles off, we could see a big enemy concentration round Msus airfield. But the squadron leader told us to wait for further orders.

Everything was quiet and peaceful and we went off on our own to investigate a deserted truck about a mile away. We were pleased to find a little tinned food and a fine pair of German gauntlets. Suddenly my driver shouted and pointed south. Moving fast over the sand towards the other two cars were two vehicles. One, with a long black barrel, was clearly a German 88 mm. From the earphones hanging over the edge of the turret came an order "*Go forward and machine gun*".

For light armoured cars an attack on a German 88 was not normally a thing to be recommended, but I was in a good position to shoot up the unprotected crew from the rear and force them to withdraw. In any case we were all heartily sick of retreating from an enemy who seemed to be having everything his own way. As soon as we were within range I gave the order to fire but after a couple of bursts a round failed to extract and the light machine gun jammed. I grabbed a cleaning rod and, climbing out on to the turret, managed to clear the obstruction in the barrel.

We began to close in at full speed and Nottingham opened fire. I could see our tracer flowing swiftly into the target in long savage bursts. The German fire was quickly silenced. But as we closed in to within 250 yards the small Besa jammed again and I then made the fatal mistake of wrestling with it instead of reloading the heavier 15 mm. This gave the remaining enemy crew their chance. With a sudden paralysing shock the turret filled with smoke, somebody cried out in pain, my left leg went numb. Jim Nottingham called "*I can't move, Sir, my legs have gone*".

Somehow we got him out and laid him on the sand. One leg was severed completely just below the knee, the other was terribly smashed. In a ridiculously calm voice I asked him how he felt and his dead white face replied "*Not so bad*". I had been hit in the knee and Robinson, my driver was wounded in the hand...

It was dark when they carried me to a small German ambulance in which I was to make the first stage of a 600 mile journey to Tripoli. When I came to we had arrived at a German field dressing station near Agedabia. In excellent English a doctor with kind eyes examined me and said that my knee should be operated on as soon as possible. But he was sorry — he had to proceed to Benghazi and hand all British wounded to the Italians.

Pain in the amputated leg

The rest of the journey was done in four stages via Agedabia, Agheila, Cirte, and Misurata. Each stage consisted of five or six hours rattling and bumping in an overcrowded ambulance without blankets and food, and frequently without water. Morphia was not given and at the end of the day, when the stretchers were carried into Red Cross tents resistance to pain was at its lowest. It was then that we were taken one by one to the operating tent where the real pain was still to come.

I was luckier than most with regard to the lack of anaesthetics. But at Misurata the doctor explained to me that he was going to cut open the back of my knee for a small operation and that, unfortunately, my heart was "*too weak to allow the use of any anaesthetic*". Four Italians then held me down while the interpreter held a mug of 'cognac' to my lips and gave a running commentary on the course of the operation in lurid American slang.

Things improved when we reached Bu Setta Hospital at Tripoli. Compared with previous field hospitals it was like a paradise. But hardly any attempt was made to get us clean and, owing to a shortage of urine bottles, eight of us were reduced to sharing a rusty jam tin. Next morning three of us — a captain in the gunners, a RAF pilot, and I — each had a leg amputated. I was the last and had a long wait in an adjoining room where I could plainly hear the previous operation in progress. For the rest of the day the pain was pretty bad, not in the stump but quite distinctly in the toes, ankle, and knee of the amputed leg. So vivid was this impression that I found myself constantly raising the bedclothes to look incredulously at the short length of white bandage stained with red that was all that remained of my leg.

We soon made many friends among the Italians, above all Sister Anna. She was the old nun in charge of our wing who looked after us with unfailing kindness. She loved to bring us specially cooked eggs and sweets and oranges and hand them to us with a sweet smile, pinching our cheeks as if we were children. We grew very fond of her and it was bitter news to hear, months later, that she had been killed in a RAF raid. It was another old nun rather like her who assured us that we were not to worry because our legs had been properly buried in the local cemetery and that "*the Lord would give them back*" to us when we died."

Interviewed recently Thurstan Brewin described how he felt when he finally crossed the Mediterranean to Caserta Hospital near Naples. There were British doctors at work and, best of all, British Red Cross parcels, cigarettes, and books. Brewin officially ran the prisoners' library — unofficially he also produced a secret news sheet with headline stories of allied successes gleaned from denials in local newspapers. His role as librarian is remembered by Captain Brian Stone in Prisoner from Alamein.

"*During the six days I was there I was able to read five books. They were brought to the bedside by an officer with one leg who combined a great knowledge of books with an extraordinary ability to carry large numbers of them whilst walking with crutches. He could run almost as fast as a complete man by hopping and using his crutches, despite being wounded only seven months before*".

For Brewin a year in Italy passed painfully slowly — even though he made many good friends from all parts of the world; learnt a lot of Italian, a little German, some French, and several card games; and enjoyed the sun and the beauty of the countryside. The whispered conversations after dark with an Italian doctor's daughter in a window some 10 feet below the ward, and the smuggled chocolate that resulted, were both a help. But Brewin hated the captivity, did not appreciate having his head shaved, and got tired of macaroni floating in greasy soup.

From prisoner to pirate

Some of the books Brewin enjoyed in captivity were on basic science, a subject he had barely touched at school — it was not then essential for entry to medical school. But while helping the captive doctors in Italy he was inspired to ask "*Can I be a doctor with only one leg?*" Presumably the answer was yes, because soon after his return to England in 1943 he started as a student at Guy's Hospital.

Apart from the doodlebug flying bombs that fell on London during his exams, Brewin remembers medical school as great fun and probably little different from student life today. And disability did not hold him back when he qualified. At Guy's he and his fellow houseman George Scott were famed for their high speed descent of five flights of stairs — one running, the other hopping. Brewin's boss Sir Rowan Boland had lost an eye in the First World War and was quite an inspiration. On one memorable ward round the doctors, one with a wooden leg, the other with a black eye patch, found themselves listening to a former merchant seaman's paranoid delusions. He thought he was being pursued by pirates. *"Let's do this properly,"* said Boland, *"on the next ward round I'll have a parrot on my shoulder"*.

Primum non nocere?

Reprinted from
The Lancet,
1994, Vol **344**, pages 1487–1488

Primum non nocere (Above all do no harm) is usually quoted by medical writers with great respect, even reverence. Gillon,[1] on the other hand, regarded the famous aphorism as virtually worthless. "Best consigned to the medical history books" was his verdict. Benefit and risk always have to be balanced, he argued, and if this principle were to govern medicine, such balancing would be prohibited. Nevertheless, uncritical adulation has continued unabated: "Our primary consideration should always be *primum non nocere*";[2] "medicine's most cherished principle — first, do no harm";[3] "a major tenet that all of us learn in medical school and that all of us try to observe in clinical practice";[4] "a dictum which has governed the practice of medicine since the time of Hippocrates";[5] and so on.

What are we to make of this? For many years, like Gillon, I was puzzled by the respect shown to a rule of thumb that felt good — because we all want to avoid needless harm — but didn't really say anything helpful. It made difficult decisions sound easy. Every time benefit and risk were weighed one against the other, the scales were supposed to tip the same way. Such extreme efforts not to risk harm could dramatically reduce benefit. However, I suggest that this famous Latin aphorism, though untenable as a strict rule, should be retained as a symbol of certain aspects of good clinical judgment.

Gillon, though he favoured abandoning *primum non nocere*, considered *non nocere* (do no harm, the so-called principle of non-malefiscence) a vital principle of medical practice.[1] Vital it may be, but surely too obvious to be of help to anyone but academic classifiers. Would anyone mad enough or evil enough to want to harm people, without thought of benefit, be put off by ethical precepts or Latin tags? Like so much fashionable medical ethics, such principles seem to me[6] — and to Mary Warnock when reviewing a book recently[7] — of little help to the practising doctor.

Should doctors knowingly risk doing more harm than good? Sometimes the media, when in critical mood and full of righteous hindsight, seem to be saying they should not. But it takes only a moment to see that such extreme caution would virtually paralyse the fight against disease and injury. Almost every effective treatment can sometimes do more harm than good. There are some ways in which medicine is different from other activities, but this isn't one of them. In economic, military, political — even personal — affairs, it is often fully realised and accepted, when a decision is made, that what is decided *could* finish up doing nothing but harm. This is a risk that is deliberately taken. There are times when every conceivable option is unattractive and it is just a matter of picking the one that seems the least unattractive.

Now try asking a friend (or a lecture audience) if it can ever be right for a doctor to do something that he or she knows will *probably* do more harm than good. Not just possibly, but probably. In my experience, almost a hundred percent of the public and many professionals will at first say "*no, that can never be right*". Yet here again it is not difficult to convince most people that they have not thought it through. If a treatment, risky or unpleasant as it is, offers the only hope, then patients and their families may badly want it, even when they know full well that the chance of worthwhile benefit is slim and the risk of side-effects very high.

Unfortunately, we never have all the evidence we would like. How sure are we that this drastic treatment offers a real chance, albeit a small one, of substantial and lasting benefit? Which do we dread most — twenty cases of serious side-effects with no benefit, or one needless death? Such evidence as there is may suggest that it has to be one or the other. And how sure are we that the situation is hopeless if we do nothing? In medicine it is hard to be sure of anything. We can only weigh the evidence; bear in mind individual lifestyle, hopes, fears, and wishes; and rely on the varying proportions of trust and informed consent that each patient seems to want or need.

Whenever a patient finishes up worse off, instead of better off, I suggest that there are three questions to be asked. Did the patient have exactly the treatment intended? Were the risks correctly assessed? And was acceptance of these risks, after a careful review of all other options, in this patient's best interests? The last question must always be considered on an individual basis. The answer will not be the same for every patient. But if the answer to all three questions is yes, then it seems to me that there is no valid reason to criticise what was done.

Primum non nocere, with its emphasis on only one side of the equation, is likely to appeal more to doves than to hawks — in other words, to those whose main fear is of the treatment being worse than the disease, rather than to those who fear failure through lack of boldness. Some feel that the famous phrase does harm by discouraging firm action. Gifford[8] points out that adverse drug effects, for example, get far more publicity than do deaths or disabilities due to lack of suffficiently aggressive treatment. The motto, he declares, is the shield of therapeutic nihilists and the battle cry of consumer advocates who think only of harm and danger.

When practising doctors quote *primum non nocere* with approval, I suggest that they have in mind five main considerations. And if they don't, perhaps they should.

First, although the rule "*above all, do no harm*" cannot be logically sustained, "*never forget the possibility that you may do more harm than good*" makes good sense. Though lacking in neatness and brevity, it could no doubt be rendered in Latin for those who love the quasi mystical authority of an ancient language. Sound clinical judgment must always give careful attention to both sides of the equation, but perhaps the emphasis on harm is justified by the fact that dangers, short term, medium term, and long term, are more likely to be neglected than are benefits. To make sure that we never forget harm, the saying reminds us to think of this first — before we get too excited about the prospect of benefit.

Second, if side-effects are not to be missed or dismissed, careful questioning of each patient is needed, during treatment and after treatment, both for their sake and for the sake of future patients. Some side-effects are obvious. Others are far from obvious and are easily missed unless this is done. Armed with such information we have to consider how much in the way of side-effects, and what sorts of side-effect, will each patient tolerate? It is also sometimes forgotten that the risks and side-effects of many treatments (eg, surgery, radiotherapy, or chemotherapy for cancer) will depend not just on whether such treatment is given, but also on how it is given — whether modestly and gently (perhaps risking failure) or aggressively (perhaps achieving more cures but with a greater risk of ill effects). There are always options within options.

Third, again taking the word *primum* as rhetorical emphasis rather than as a literal demand for priority, *primum non nocere* stresses the need for more formal studies of the harmful side of the equation. Randomised trials are usually thought of either as research or as the best method to assess benefit. But they are also the best method to assess harm. For example, results in breast and rectal cancer, after more than fifty years of drastic surgery, have been no less good since the operations became less radical.[9] Randomised comparisons of outcome from the start[10,11] would have prevented this serious error.

Fourth, *primum non nocere* is saying to us that if a treatment is unlikely to make much difference, apart from its placebo effect, then to risk doing serious harm is hard to justify. This is especially true in two very different circumstances. One is where the condition is not serious and probably self-limiting. The other is where the condition is grave and probably incurable. Here the danger is that we make the mistake that military strategists call reinforcing failure. Or that we embark on something desperate for no other reason than that the situation is desperate. It is often easier to do something than to do nothing. To let events take their course may demand both greater confidence and greater communication skills.

Finally, *primum non nocere* reminds us that the gut feeling of many people is to be especially unhappy about any death or disability that is caused by treatment. The emotional impact of such a death may be so strong that logic becomes a casualty. Many people will be less shocked by several "natural" deaths (natural meaning due to the disease or injury) than by one "unnatural" one — a death inflicted not by nature but by man. So it may not always be wise to follow the simple logic that argues for whichever policy leads to the lowest total number of deaths.

Taken as a rigid rule, *primum non nocere* does not stand up to criticism, but perhaps it is worth preserving as a symbol of these five facets of sound clinical judgment.

References

1. Gillon R. "Primum non nocere" and the principle of non-malefiscence. *BMJ* 1985; **291**: 130–31.

2. Miller WT. Primum non nocere. *Semin Roentgenol* 1993; **28**: 291–92.

3. Goodyear-Smith F. Political correction or primum non nocere? *N Z Med J* 1993; **106**: 416.

4. Eisdorfer C, Kessler DA, Spector AN, eds. Caring for the elderly. Baltimore: Johns Hopkins University Press, 1989.

5. Brouillette JN. Primum non nocere. *J Florida Med Assoc* 1991; **78**: 527–28.

6. Brewin TB. How much ethics is needed to make a good doctor? *Lancet* 1993; **341**: 161–63.

7. Warnock M. [Book review] *BMJ* 1994; **308**: 988–89.

8. Gifford RW. Primum non nocere. *JAMA* 1977; **238**: 589–90.

9. Bailey and Love's short practice of surgery. 21st ed. London: Chapman & Hall, 1992.

10. Bradford Hill A. Medical ethics and controlled trials. *BMJ* 1963; **i**: 1043–49.

11. Chalmers TC. Randomization of the first patient. *Med Clin N Am* 1975; **59**: 1035–38.

Appetite perversions and taste changes triggered or abolished by radiotherapy (Abstract)

Reprinted from
Clinical Radiology, 1982, Vol 33, pages 471–475

Special questioning of 819 oncology patients whose treatment included radiotherapy has revealed 147 instances where local tumour radiation — apparently regardless of tumour type, site, or volume radiated — has either triggered (97 cases) or abolished (50 cases) an isolated appetite perversion. Both effects typically occur when a dose of about 500-1500 cGy has been reached and at a stage when little, if any, tumour regression is evident. No correlation can be seen with anorexia or with the usually recognised side effects of radiotherapy. Spontaneous return to normal is quite common in cases triggered by tumour treatment, but rare in cases starting before diagnosis. The latter may cease when the tumour is treated. The explanation for these highly selective and rapidly reversible aversions or cravings is totally obscure, but questioning large numbers of patients has provided certain clues, including frequent descriptions of an underlying change in taste or odour and also close links with two other equally unexplained phenomena—(1) alcohol intolerance in tumour patients and (2) the cravings and aversions of pregnancy.

Can a tumour cause the same appetite perversion or taste change as a pregnancy?

Reprinted from
The Lancet,
1980, Vol ii, pages 907–908

Summary

24 women experienced in later life the same craving or aversion as they had experienced in pregnancy (or an opposite feeling for the same substance). Most cases were associated with a tumour or its treatment.

Introduction

Interviews with 1237 hospital patients (850 attending a radiotherapy and oncology centre, the rest inpatients with no overt tumour) have revealed many isolated and bizarre appetite perversions in both men and women. Some were triggered by tumour treatment; others started several years before diagnosis, then ceased when a tumour was removed or irradiated. 462 of the women had experienced cravings and aversions in 40% of their pregnancies. 24 of these women, who form the subject of this report, had in later life the same craving or aversion as they had experienced in pregnancy or the opposite feeling for the same substance. Usually the appetite perversion was associated with a tumour or its treatment.

Most cases seem to be mediated by a specific taste change (STC) or a reversible change in the odour of a particular substance (everything else tasting and smelling normal). In this report STC is used for all unconditioned cravings and aversions, whether in pregnancy or not.

Of 24 women (mean age 51, range 37–73) who described the return in later life of an STC identical or opposite to that experienced in one or more of their pregnancies, 22 had the following tumours: carcinoma of cervix (7), breast (5), ovary (4), endometrium (1), vulva (1), bladder (1), bronchus (1), sarcoma of uterus (1), astrocytoma (1). The other 2 had no overt tumour: 1 had cone biopsy of cervix for chronic cervicitis (the only abnormality subsequently seen histologically), and the other had a grade 4 smear suggesting malignant change in the cervix, but no in-situ or invasive changes were found in the hysterectomy specimen.

Edible substances involved were tea (7 patients); anything sweet (3); ice-cream (2); coffee, egg, potato, pickled onion, milk, cheese, fried food, soup, fruit cake, oatmeal, milk pudding, oranges, and gooseberries (1 each). Inedible substances were tobacco smoke (2 cases), coal (1), and perfume (1). The total number of substances is 29, because in 5 of the 24 cases two substances were involved. With 18 substances the symptom in both pregnancy and later life was aversion; with 7 it was craving; with 3 it was craving in pregnancy but aversion in later life; and with 1 vice versa.

Radiotherapy to the tumour triggered the onset of STC in 9 cases; tumour surgery did so in 4; in 1 it seemed to start the day before surgery. In 9 cases STC started between 1 month and 10 years before diagnosis (mean $3\frac{1}{2}$ years); and in the 6 cases where clear evidence is available, tumour treatment abolished it in 3. Finally, in 1 patient symptoms started 8 months before the recurrence of a tumour became clinically evident.

Examples

1. A patient disliked tea when pregnant and again at the age of 59. Surgery for carcinoma of cervix 7 years later made no difference, but radium implant for a vaginal metastasis restored normal enjoyment.

2. The smell of cigarette smoke and the taste of tea, both of which were repugnant to a patient in her first pregnancy (but not in her next three pregnancies) were again very repugnant for 4 months before both were abolished by pre-operative radiation for endometrial carcinoma.

3. Aversion for ice-cream in 5 out of 7 pregnancies was followed by craving for it for a year before diagnosis of carcinoma of cervix.

4. A farmer's wife found that surgery for ovarian carcinoma triggered the same change in the smell and taste of coffee that she had experienced in pregnancy; it lasted 3 months.

5. The patient mentioned above with the grade-4 cervical smear ate coal in all her six pregnancies and again for 3 weeks after hysterectomy.

6. Tea tasted *"like some terrible poison"* in pregnancy and for 3 months after the first few days of each of two courses of radiotherapy for breast cancer, the first postoperative to the chest wall, the second 3 years later for brain metastases.

Discussion

The well-known but never explained cravings and aversions of pregnant women[1] are usually thought of as peculiar to pregnancy — at least so far as edible substances are concerned. But the 24 case-histories reported here are supported by a long-term study with many other cases that are indistinguishable from them except that the substance concerned is not the same as in pregnancy. Similarities between pregnancy STC and non-pregnancy STC include: (i) the same remarkable specificity in many cases — with eggs, for example, the yolk may be the only part affected, or just the white, or just boiled eggs, not scrambled or fried, or vice versa; (ii) the same lack of any correlation with anorexia or gastrointestinal disease; (iii) the same wide variety of substances (though there are significant differences as well as similarities in the frequency of the more common ones); (iv) the same clear descriptions by many patients of a persistent change in the smell or taste of a substance, which suddenly becomes very unpleasant, very enticing, or very dull, all other tastes and smells remaining unaffected; (v) the same instant recovery of normal smell or taste when a child is born or a tumour removed or irradiated; (vi) the same cravings as well as aversions, though cravings are less common and less strong in non-pregnancy STC; (vii) the same majority of cases in which a single substance is involved, the same minority involving two or very occasionally more; and (viii) the same frequent descriptions of 'rebound' — abolition of a craving being followed for a week or two, sometimes longer, by a strong aversion to the same substance, or vice versa, then the return of normal taste.

A separate question is the evidence for a link with tumours. Non-pregnancy STC is not confined to patients with tumours; but nor are many well-recognised tumour syndromes. The 3 cases reported in which STC was abolished by local tumour treatment are supported by 75 other examples of this in the unpublished series (STC often being present for several years before being abolished in this way) and by 197 cases of triggering of STC by local tumour treatment. But are these effects dependent on the presence of tumour in the treated area? To help answer this question patients were asked about their whole life, including all surgical operations. The incidence of abolition and triggering was significantly lower in non-tumour surgery.

Taste[2] and odour[3] changes have been studied in cancer patients, but mainly from a nutritional angle and in relation to aversions that might explain cancer anorexia; using taste testing rather than questioning; and probably not detecting — or not taking seriously — many of the bizarre and highly selective aversions and cravings discussed in the present report.

Non-pregnancy STC (like alcohol intolerance, which in several respects it resembles[4,5]) is a convincing clinical entity yet often seems — to the patient as well as the doctor — irrelevant and absurd. Any nutritional significance seems unlikely, especially since tobacco and inedible substances are often involved. But this symptom could be *"trying to tell us something"* — perhaps about oncofetal antigens and the immunology of pregnancy and of tumours; perhaps about some quite different and undiscovered aspect of normal or abnormal growth control.

References

1. Trethowan WH, Dickens G. Cravings, aversions and pica of pregnancy. In: Howells JG, ed. Modern perspectives in psycho-obstetrics. Edinburgh: Oliver and Boyd, 1972: 251–68.

2. De Wys WD. Changes in taste sensation and feeding behaviour in cancer patients: a review. *J Hum Nutr* 1978; **32:** 447–53.

3. Nielsen SS, Theologides A, Vickers ZM. Influence of food odors and food aversions and preferences in patients with cancer. *Am J Clin Nutr* (in press).

4. Brewin TB. Alcohol shift and alcohol dysphagia in Hodgkin's disease, carcinoma of cervix and other neoplasms. *Br J Cancer* 1966; **20:** 688–702.

5. Brewin TB. The incidence of alcohol intolerance in women with tumours of uterus, ovary or breast. *Proc Roy Soc Med* 1967; **80:** 1308–09.

Alcohol intolerance in cancer – summaries of three studies

The incidence of alcohol intolerance in women with tumours of the uterus, ovary or breast (Summary)

Reprinted from
Proceedings of the Royal Society of Medicine, 1967,
Vol 60, pages 1308–1309

The paper of James *et al* (1957) was followed by other reports of alcohol pain in carcinoma, including cervix (Healy 1959), uterine body (Bichel 1959) and breast (Braun & Schnider 1958). This symptom has also been described in lesions showing no evidence of neoplastic change (Alexander 1953, Conn 1957), while slight pain, often in the shoulders and arms, is one of the features of an apparently harmless alcohol syndrome that affects some people all their lives (Conn 1957, and 1966, personal communication, Snell 1966, Brewin 1966b). Bichel (1959) made a plea for the recognition of other kinds of alcohol intolerance (nausea, dyspnoea, flushing and so on), but considered that these symptoms, like alcohol pain, occurred mainly in Hodgkin's disease. Recent evidence (Brewin 1966a, c) suggests widespread intolerance in neoplastic disease, including not only obviously abnormal effects (such as pain or bleeding at a site of disease, or bizarre attacks of systemic distress, after very small amounts of alcohol), but also unexplained loss of desire for alcohol, perversion of smell or taste, burning dysphagia in spite of dilution, and lowering of threshold for normal intoxicating and hangover effects. A single pathogenesis, responsible for all these effects, is suggested by the many features which they share, including lack of any correlation with tumour site or spread, frequent onset long before diagnosis, occasional transient appearance at the time of treatment, the same uneven pattern of disease incidence, and the same instances of immediate return to normal tolerance, or shift to a new kind of intolerance, with modest doses of radiotherapy or certain drugs.

Table 1
Incidence of alcohol intolerance in 332 women with neoplastic disease

Site of disease	Total cases	Cases showing alcohol intolerance	
		No.	%
Uterine cervix	106	64	60
Uterine body	58	23	40
Ovary	61	17	28
Breast	107	16	15

The incidence found in tumours of the uterine body is not significantly different from that found in tumours of the ovary (P>0.05)

Table 1 shows the result of a new survey, involving 332 women not used in previous estimates of incidence, and based mainly on the taking of a very careful history in every case. The most striking finding is a much higher incidence of alcohol intolerance among 106 women with cervical carcinoma than among 107 women with breast carcinoma. It is thought that this difference is real, since both groups came from the same geographical area, contained the same proportion of 'drinkers'* (cervix 54%, breast 57%), had a similar average prognosis, with many early as well as late cases, and were questioned in exactly the same way by the same observer, who was equally interested in both diseases and had no working hypothesis or conscious bias of any kind. Table 2 shows that the difference is as true of changes in taste or threshold as it is of pain or other frankly abnormal effect.

Assessment may be difficult, especially when a patient is not prepared to risk further alcohol after a single incident. Cases where there was any doubt were fully documented, then classified on the spot as 'probable' or

---

* 'Drinkers': patients normally unlikely to go more than 2 months without tasting alcohol. 'Regular drinkers': patients normally unlikely to go more than a week without tasting alcohol

'possible' without regard to time of onset or probability of being related to the disease. 'Probable' cases were later found to be more than 3 times as common in the cervix group (cervix 27, breast 8) and were accepted. 'Possible' cases were all rejected.

Table 2
Incidence of different types of alcohol intolerance in 106 women with carcinoma of cervix and 107 women with carcinoma of breast

| Site of disease | *Type of intolerance* | | | | | | *Lowered threshold* | |
	Pain	*Bleeding*	*Attacks*	*Other abnormal effects*	*Loss of desire for alcohol*	*Change in taste or dysphagia*	*Intoxification, hangover*	*Gastro-intestinal*
Cervix	10	4	27	7	12	11	11	17
Breast	1	-	2	4	1	2	3	6

Figures represent actual number of patients experiencing each type of intolerance. Some experienced more than one kind, either concurrently or as a result of a 'shift'. Loss of desire or distaste attributable to anorexia, or to previous alcohol symptoms, is excluded

The incidence is as high as that previously found to apply only to 'regular drinkers' (Brewin 1966a). This appears to be due mainly to the use of even greater care and tact when taking the history, with absolute privacy in every case and a consistent policy of continuing to talk for several minutes to any patient who initially denied intolerance or said that she did not take alcohol; paying particular attention to family celebrations, toasts at weddings or christenings, and to medicinal use, yet avoiding leading questions about specific types of intolerance. As a result, the incidence in regular drinkers shows no significant difference (cervix 12 out of 17 in the new series, 10 out of 19 in the old; breast 3 out of 20, previously 2 out of 20), whereas the incidence in those not in the 'drinkers' category shows a remarkable change (cervix now 25 out of 49, previously 1 out of 34).

The proportion of cervix and breast cases showing either a local effect at the tumour site, abolition of intolerance by radiotherapy or surgery, or onset within a 3-year period before or after diagnosis, is not significantly different (cervix 50 out of 64, breast 10 out of 16: $P > 0.05$). Very few of the other cases show any positive suggestion of not being similarly related to the tumour, evidence being frequently lacking due to a natural reluctance to resume alcohol.

Of the 54 cervix patients whose intolerance was present before diagnosis, 36 (67%) had experienced it for more than a year, including 20 (37 %) for more than 3 years. Of 34 Stage 1 cases, 14 showed intolerance. Of 8 carcinoma-in-situ, 4 showed it. In theory, therefore, these reactions to alcohol could make a significant contribution to earlier diagnosis. Although there are many other causes, some benign, it would seem sensible for any woman who develops alcohol intolerance to have at least a clinical and cytological check on her cervix.

References

Alexander DA (1953) *Brit. med. J.* ii, 1376

Bichel J (1959) *Acta med. scand.* **164**, 105

Braun WE & Schnider BI (1958) *J. Amer. med. Ass.* **168**, 1882

Brewin TB (1966a) *Brit. med. J.* ii, 437

(1966b) *Brit. med. J.* ii, 1322

(1966c) *Brit. J. Cancer* **20**, 688

Conn HO (1957) *Arch intern. med.* **100**, 241

Healy JB (1959) *Lancet* ii, 296

James A H, Harley H R, Horton E H & Storring F K (1957) *Lancet* i, 299

Snell WE (1966) *Brit. med. J.* ii, 645

Alcohol shift and alcohol dysphagia in Hodgkin's disease, carcinoma of cervix and other neoplasms (Summary)

Reprinted from
The British Journal of Cancer,
1966, Vol **XX**, pages 688–702

In Hodgkin's disease, carcinoma of cervix, and other neoplasms, intolerance to alcohol may present in a variety of ways, of which alcohol pain is only one. The term alcohol shift is suggested for the ceasing of one kind of intolerance, usually as a result of local radiotherapy, and its immediate replacement by another. This has been seen 40 times in 33 patients. The new effect may be alcohol pain at a focus of disease which has not previously given rise to this symptom, or it may be systemic alcohol symptoms, such as abnormal vomiting, headache, or flushing, never before experienced. On a further 22 occasions similar alcohol effects have occurred for the first time during or immediately after the treatment of patients who had been tolerating alcohol normally when they had last taken it.

Regardless of dissemination of the disease only one focus normally gives rise to alcohol intolerance, but during a shift multiple alcohol pains may occur, indicating areas of involvement before they are otherwise detectable. In Hodgkin's disease tender nodes may appear at a new site of alcohol pain immediately after the shift.

Alcohol Dysphagia is the term suggested when the oropharynx or oesophagus or both, though showing no evidence of disease, give rise to abnormal symptoms, usually a burning sensation, while alcohol is being swallowed. This symptom, which has been observed in 21 patients with various neoplasms, may disappear when radiotherapy is given to a distant neoplastic focus, for example a carcinoma of cervix. Like other forms of systemic alcohol intolerance its onset may be long before diagnosis, or it may appear for the first time much later, sometimes as a transient effect after treatment or during an alcohol shift.

The possible significance of these clinical observations is discussed.

I am indebted to many colleagues, not only in Glasgow, but at Guy's Hospital (where my interest in alcohol pain began in 1953), Westminster Hospital, and the Hamilton clinic of the Ontario Cancer Foundation. I owe a special debt to all those patients with alcohol intolerance who agreed to risk, or to suffer, transient unpleasant effects, in the hope that something might be learned that would help others.

Alcohol intolerance in neoplastic disease (Summary)

Reprinted from
the British Medical Journal
1966, Vol 2, pages 437–441

After rejection of 33 doubtful cases, 155 cases of alcohol intolerance are presented; 60 patients had Hodgkin's disease, 24 had other lymphoid disorders, 16 had carcinoma of the cervix, and 55 had a wide variety of other tumours, at least three of them benign. Alcohol caused pain at a site of disease in 79 cases, bleeding in 14, and severe generalized symptoms ('alcohol attacks') in 18. Other effects are described. Controlled capsule experiments have shown that 1 ml of alcohol may be sufficient. Reasons are given to justify the inclusion of 46 patients showing only distaste for alcohol or a lowered threshold for its more normal effects.

It has been found that any of these forms of intolerance may (1) appear as a very early symptom of local neoplastic change; (2) disappear after fairly small doses of radiotherapy to a focus of disease, quite insufficient to eradicate the latter; and (3) be suppressed by small doses of cytotoxic drugs, anti-histamines, corticosteroids, or phenylbutazone.

From the questioning of 360 patients with lymphoid tumours and 700 patients with other neoplasms it is suggested that alcohol intolerance is not uncommon in several apparently unrelated neoplastic conditions. In others typical cases occur, but only infrequently. In the lymphoid series intolerance is more common in women.

Are there two kinds of ward round?

Reprinted from
the British Medical Journal,
1982, Vol 285, pages 1765–1766

The scene could be any medical or surgical ward anywhere. Discussion of an interesting diagnostic problem (out of earshot of the patients) is just coming to an end...

CONSULTANT:
Are we agreed then? The diagnosis is wide open, and we take no further action until we have the results of the various x-rays and so on.... Now, it is getting late, who do we see next?

YOUNG DOCTOR (*new to team*):
I think we can probably skip the next two cases, they are both terminal. There's really nothing anyone can do. The first is the 64-year-old man with widespread secondary carcinoma from an unknown primary, who has been blocking a bed for a month. He continues to deteriorate. The other man is 72 and...

CONSULTANT (*interrupting*):
Hold on a minute. If the first man you are talking about is George Reid, the plumber, it depends what you mean by 'deteriorating'. When I last saw him he was getting weaker, but we had had quite a lot of success with various symptoms and he was much happier. What's the present position?

YOUNG DOCTOR:
The present position? Well, it has been known for some time that he has multiple liver and bone metastases. Shall I repeat his scans? They don't seem to have been done for over two months.

CONSULTANT (*quietly, after a pause*):
Have you taken a history?

YOUNG DOCTOR (*puzzled*):
Taken a history? I don't understand…I thought we were talking about Mr Reid.

CONSULTANT:
We are. Each ward round we need you to tell us how he is getting on. Has there been any return of pain or shortness of breath? Is his morale better, or worse, or about the same? If he has a new pain of a different type you will have to take an especially careful history. Does it arise from a bone metastasis or could there be some other cause? Has he any nausea? If so, is it due to his liver metastases? To some drug we are giving him? Perhaps to some needless fear or conflict that we might be able to resolve? With a differential diagnosis like that, repeating scans is about as much use as cold tea on a wet Sunday.

WARD SISTER:
Perhaps I can help. He is still losing weight, and he is not quite so keen now to leave his bed to watch television with the others. But there has been no return of his original symptoms. In fact he has been joking with the nurses and is really in remarkably good form, especially since the horse he fancied came in second in the Derby and he won £10.

CONSULTANT:
Good for him…I must ask his advice sometimes…(*he turns to a 30-year-old doctor who has been with the team for two years*)…Alan, we've got medical students coming tomorrow, haven't we? Could you take them? I suggest you first discuss the previous patient in detail, including all the investigations we are going to do. Then take them to George Reid. Tell them how we got his pain under control. Confess how slow we were to realise that his attacks of 'shortness of breath' were due to hyperventilation. See how many of them remember the biochemistry of overbreathing. Remind them that this sometimes happens to people under stress. Point out that he has been free of attacks since we explained it all to him. Incidentally he had oral thrush, didn't he? Or was that another patient? Anyway, tell them it's a sign of professional incompetence to miss this in terminal patients.

WARD SISTER:
Before we talk about the next patient could I ask you two questions about George Reid? Can he go for a short drive in his son's new car?…Good… And could he see you alone for a minute some time?

CONSULTANT:
Of course. Will 5.30 tomorrow be soon enough? I'm afraid I'm very tied up till

then. Now let's hear about the 72-year-old man you mentioned who has just come into the next bed...Alan, you admitted him, tell us about him. Just a quick summary of the main points because it is getting late. A bit about his background and his job before he retired. How certain is the diagnosis and are we really sure it's terminal? Then his symptoms. Are they all due to his malignant disease? Which of them worries him most? Do we need specialist help with any of them? Finally, the main points of your provisional plan for him...

*   *   *   *

Ten minutes later the ward round has seen George Reid and the new patient, who are now alone together.

GEORGE:
Bill? You know what I think? I think there are two kinds of ward round.

BILL:
How do you mean — two kinds?

GEORGE:
I've been in five or six different hospital wards in the past two years — and a few more before that. I've talked to other patients. I've seen the difference. One kind of ward round is interested only in certain patients, the other is interested in every patient. When the first kind gets to someone like you or me, they either go straight on to the next patient — with maybe a quick nod if you're lucky — or they come and see you, but they do it in a quiet, awkward, switched-off sort of way. They don't really get to grips with any of your problems. It's almost as if, to them, you had...how can I put it...sort of died already, and it's all very sad, but there's no more to be said. So, of course, when they've gone, you feel even more depressed than you did before the ward round began. The other kind treats every patient as a real live person, until proved otherwise...with opinions and feelings...hopes and doubts...good days and bad days...maybe even a sense of humour. Take this ward round we have just had. He shook your hand as if he meant it, didn't he? You got the feeling he was just as glad to see you as to see any other patient in the ward. He had heard about the boxing you did when you were in the Navy. Not like some wards where they seem to think you have been old all your life. Then he noticed your address — and asked you if it was true that the pub at the end of your road had changed hands. It didn't take a minute and it helped, didn't it? You felt human — a person, not just a piece of the furniture — or, worse still, an embarrassment to everyone, like a bad smell in a clean ward. Last week he told me the story of the guide at Niagara Falls, who says, *"I'll bet you have*

nothing like this where you come from," and the little man from Glasgow who replies "*No, but I know a good plumber who might be able to fix it for you.*" I had heard it before, but I didn't have the heart to tell him so; he must have saved it up for the ward round, knowing I was a plumber. So that's the first thing you get on a good ward round. They treat you like a human being. And you begin to relax a little. And you feel less tense, more yourself.

BILL:
What's the second thing?

GEORGE:
The second thing is that they want to know all about your symptoms. The ones that matter most to you are the ones that matter most to them. So far as possible, they aim to do something about them. There's nothing half-hearted about it. You can see they mean business. They have a quick look at you, check up on a few things in a professional, workmanlike sort of way — maybe explain some of your symptoms — and then tell you what they are going to do and what they are hoping for.

BILL:
Perhaps in some wards they just don't have the time. It's like any other job. You have to pick and choose a bit when you are under pressure.

GEORGE:
No. It's not that. Take this lot we are with now. Every week they have a dozen new acute cases — sometimes they hardly know if they are coming or going. At times like that they can't spend more than a minute or two with patients like you and me. Even when they are not so busy, they forget things, they make mistakes, they are not perfect…far from it. But they care. They try. They don't give up easily. When I came in I was in a terrible state, with pain and shortness of breath and God knows what else. I wanted to feel better quickly or die. And they saw this immediately. So they got to work. No messing about. No red tape. No waiting for scans or x-rays that weren't really needed. It took them less than two days to discover I needed four times the normal dose of morphine. That's quite common apparently. They asked me if I preferred tablets or liquid, and they explained that once the correct dose is found, then that's it — it doesn't usually lose its effect, and there's no need to increase the dose. Sometimes you can reduce it later on.

BILL:
Maybe they think there's nothing they can do for some people and they'd just be wasting their time.

24

GEORGE:
Well, if they think that, they have got it wrong, haven't they? Any doctor who thinks that is only half a doctor. If a patient is really suffering a good doctor can always do something. I've seen it. Many times. Just taking an interest and trying something — anything — will help. And anyway a doctor's got to be sure that there isn't something crying out to be done that he didn't spot at first. I know that from my own job. You can't tell until you've weighed up a situation — and that takes a bit of skill and experience. You learn from your mistakes. You never stop learning. You enjoy life more if you approach all your work in that way — not just some of it. I get a lot of satisfaction from installing new bathrooms — that's my special interest and that's how I spend most of my time. But I'd be ashamed if I couldn't also make a good job of patching up a leak or unblocking a waste pipe for some old person living alone in a house soon due for demolition. And doing it quickly — no fuss, no frills, no unnecessary disturbance. A good plumber takes a pride in both kinds of work. He knows that either can be done well or done badly. I thought of that when the ward sister here got me unblocked last month. I never thought of a woman as a plumber, but she'd make a good one. I told her so. She did it gently, too. And what a difference it made...you would never believe what a difference it made...

BILL:
Maybe you should have been a doctor, not a plumber.

GEORGE (*smiling*):
Maybe I should...maybe I should...but I'm not complaining, I've had a good life...anyway, you'll be glad to hear that's the end of my lecture for today ... so let's see if there's anything worth listening to on the radio, shall we?

The cancer patient: communication and morale

Reprinted from
the British Medical Journal,
1977, Vol 2, pages 1623–1627

Good communication in any serious or potentially serious situation is a complex and difficult art, full of paradox. Many of those who are best at it never analyse what they do, let alone write about it. Some think that the subject cannot be taught, being dependent only on personality and experience, perhaps fostered by example. As with leadership, the essence of a good relationship between doctor and patient or nurse and patient tends to evaporate as soon as any attempt is made to put it into cold print. Warmth, concern, sincerity, and spontaneity, all so important, are inevitably diminished by anything savouring of tactics or technique. With cancer there are additional difficulties due to deep-seated fears of a special kind not encountered in any other disease (or, more correctly, group of diseases), even when closely matched in terms of symptoms and prognosis.

Many of those who have given their views have been psychiatrists or social workers — external assessors, so to speak, with all the advantages and disadvantages that this implies. Others have written only of the dying patient. Those of us directly concerned with the treatment and long-term follow-up of many patients with cancer of different kinds (some curable, some in relapse, some in remission) have had much less to say. One thing is certain. Whoever writes on this subject is walking into a minefield of misunderstandings. Some will always be determined to label him (on the basis of selective quotation) as one who 'believes that patients should be told the truth' or as one who 'believes that they should not'. We are all supposed to belong to one school or the other. Yet most of us have learnt that there are important exceptions to every generalisation and that, as Bernard Shaw said in another context *"the only golden rule is that there are no golden rules."* Every time we say *"some patients"* or *"most doctors"*, we want to add *"but by no means all"* and to give examples. Oversimplification and apparent contradictions are inevitable. This is also a very emotional subject. Strong objections raised are as likely to be due to dislike of the words or phrases used (no matter how liberally we sprinkle them with apologetic quotation marks) as to genuine disagreement with what is done.

But there is one overriding reason for not keeping silent — the importance of the subject. To anyone interested in the whole patient (as we are all taught to be from our earliest days as medical students) good communication is far from being just a fringe benefit. Sometimes it is more important than anything else. And it need not always take up a lot of time. Some authors seem to think that little can be done without fairly long interviews. Many of the rest of us, unable or unwilling to allot so much precious time to this particular aspect of our work, except with occasional patients (and by no means convinced that a long formal interview is always the best thing), are constantly impressed by the difference that a few words of the right kind at the right time can make to the morale of a frightened or depressed patient.

Background communication

Patients who feel they are *"not being told enough"* are often suffering from a feeling of insecurity due, not to insufficient frankness about their exact diagnosis or their long-term prognosis, but to lack of sustained professional interest in their symptoms, lack of good care, or lack of information about what is going on and what to expect in the immediate future. It is important always to have a plan and to tell the patient what it is. In the advanced case, if there is a reasonable chance of achieving one or more short-term objectives (less pain, easier breathing, a better night's sleep), this needs to be explained to the patient in a suitably positive and optimistic way. Seldom, if ever, is it true to say that *"nothing can be done"*.

Being a good listener need not necessarily take more than a few minutes. The main thing is to be interested, not only in all current symptoms (whether or not they make sense or seem relevant), but also in the patient as a person in his own right, who — to use Cicely Saunders' phrase — *"happens to have cancer"*[1]. If he is weak or elderly, this sort of respect for the patient, with a brief word or two about his past life or his present opinion about what is going on in the world, is especially important, as it counteracts the indignity that so often accompanies serious illness and, combined with technical efficiency, helps to reassure him that he is in good hands[2].

Some valuable forms of communication depend on good timing and on the personality of the doctor or nurse for their success. A sense of humour (which Sir Robert Hutchison[3] described as *"the same thing as a sense of proportion"*) has remarkable power to reassure, encourage, and give a feeling of security. Equally useful is irrelevant small talk about nothing in particular — the weather, football, weddings, grandchildren. This might seem quite out of place in a serious situation, or a waste of skilled time, but it is often neither, being capable of raising morale and reducing fear to a surprising degree. Why not have someone else do it? Because this would not have the same effect. Even in the most specialised clinical records, brief reminders of 'irrelevant' details in the patient's past or present life deserve quite a high priority.

Unspoken communication may have a greater impact than words. The patient may quickly decide, sometimes from little more than a smile or the firm touch of a hand, that the person speaking to him wants to help; knows how to; and has at least some idea of how he feels. Even the busiest doctor has to try to appear relaxed, unhurried and, above all, in a serious situation, not embarrassed or afraid, and very willing to answer any questions. He must be glad to see the patient. To deny the patient with cancer (whether the outlook is good or bad) the humour, good fellowship, and gossip that he could expect if he did not have cancer, serves only to increase his sense of isolation. It would be hard to exaggerate the importance of these various forms of basic background communication. The effect of what is said — or not said — about diagnosis and prognosis may depend on them.

Adapting to different situations

Sometimes communication with the cancer patient is discussed as if there was only one prognosis (hopeless from the start) and only one kind of patient (male, middle-aged, with *"affairs to settle"*, and asking for full details of his diagnosis and prognosis). Many patients with cancer feel and look well. Such patients may have a good, poor, or 50–50 chance of escaping recurrence either within the next two years or within the next 20 years. The variation in prognosis is considerable. Much misunderstanding arises when the layman believes that the doctor always knows what is going to happen. If recurrence occurs, it may be surprisingly helpful to assure the patient and his relatives that nobody 'knew' this was going to occur; it had been hoped it would not.

Even patients with advanced cancer (perhaps with distant metastases) often remain in good health for many months or even years, especially in certain kinds of cancer (breast, prostate, kidney, lymphoma, and so on) and especially if there is no weakness or loss of weight. Others are obviously ill, and may never be well again, but not all such patients should be described as 'dying'. Some would be better described as 'probably dying' or 'possibly dying'. Surprises are quite common. Finally, many patients are elderly and have other medical problems which may be just as likely as their cancer to reduce the duration of their old age.

So much for the disease. What of the patient? Most doctors will regard it as part of the art of being a good doctor that they do not hand out to every patient the same 'take it or leave it' policy when they communicate diagnosis or prognosis. They prefer to adapt, as best they can, to his personality and background and to what seems to be going on in his mind. They want to get on the same wavelength. They cannot give maximum help unless they do. But this is not easy. We cannot read the patient's thoughts. Sometimes a word with husband, wife, or close friend may be very helpful, but quite often, even in a close and happy marriage, the marriage partner is as much in the dark on this point as the doctor. Even the patient himself is sometimes not sure exactly what he fears, or what he already knows, or suspects, or wants to know, about the seriousness of his condition.

Doctors with psychiatric training often advise direct questions, inviting patients to say what they are afraid of, or how serious they think their condition is. Rightly or wrongly, many of us without such training are reluctant to do this routinely. We have known occasions where such questions were exactly what was needed, but in many cases we fear we may do more harm than good. Often it seems to us slightly impertinent; robbing the patient of some of his self respect, treading where we have no right to tread, perhaps knocking down fragile defence mechanisms as we go. We also feel that the patient's answer to a direct question is often a poor guide to the best way of helping him.

The patient's attitude

Any classification must be very crude, but at least five different situations are commonly encountered.

    (1)   The patient desperately hopes for reassurance that he or she has not '*got cancer*', or that the outlook is not hopeless.

(2)   Aggressively cheerful optimism. Clearly the patient will be deeply upset, or angry, or both, if he is bluntly given a diagnosis or prognosis that he is striving to reject.

(3)   Apparently he wants '*the full facts*', as given to relatives. If the prognosis is bad, several questions may now need rapid assessment Are there special reasons why this patient needs to have bluntly spelt out to him the worst that could happen? Will he be able to distinguish between such very different opinions as possibly only a few months (or years as the case may be) to live, and probably only a few months (or years) to live? To many patients there is little difference, both are a death sentence. Finally, is he likely to appreciate guarded optimism? Or to despise it?

(4)   This patient does not want to discuss diagnosis or prognosis. She is often living from day to day, perhaps cheerful, perhaps sad, but reasonably philosophical and relaxed, confident that everything possible is being done; maybe weak and ill; maybe frail and elderly; often not wanting to regard this particular illness as different from any other; and above all, far more concerned with immediate needs and fears than with diagnostic labels or long-range forecasts.

(5)   Tense and suspicious that they are being kept in the dark, some patients badly need more information. This must be recognised and dealt with, but it is a mistake to think that such patients must be told everything or they will continue to worry. This may be so, but it is often not so. Sometimes morale may be dramatically restored by limited explanation (anatomical rather than pathological) and encouragement. In suitable cases, show the patient his x-rays; explain to him, as to a medical student, how (for example) enlarged hilar nodes are preventing air from getting into one of his lungs and how it is hoped (by radiotherapy or chemotherapy) to get the lung working again and thus relieve his shortness of breath. If his voice is hoarse because of recurrent laryngeal nerve palsy, or if a glance at his eyes shows Horner's syndrome, explain this, too. Talk to the right kind of patient in the right kind of way and he will be interested, less afraid, and perhaps greatly reassured to know that there is no disease in his throat or eyes and that these syndromes are understood; quite common (but interesting, no

> two cases being exactly alike); harmless in themselves; and
> unlikely to get any worse.

Although the dilemma is sometimes very real and it is difficult to know what to do for the best, in many of these situations there is scarcely any choice, unless we are to be exceedingly heartless, or unless we use so many technical words or so many euphemisms that our claim to have "*told the patient*" could equally well be described as "*not telling the patient*". Those who say (and like to think) that they are "*honest with their patients and tell them the truth*" may well finish up handling the situation in exactly the same way as those who feel it is "*generally wiser not to tell patients outright*". Are we to press information on patients who do not seem to want it? Sometimes a vital clue is not the patient's first question, but his second question (or the absence of a second question), after we have begun to give him some explanation of what is going on, watching to see how he takes it. The patient, in fact, often guides us as to what we should say[4,5]. It may be difficult for some to appreciate quite what this means, but with experience its essential truth becomes clear.

Finally, either the prognosis, or the attitude of the patient, or both, may at any time change completely, so that the doctor may be confronted by a situation quite different from the one he faced initially. Communication of diagnosis and prognosis is not a dilemma to be faced once and then forgotten. It is a matter for continuous care and sensitivity in changing circumstances.

Hope and 'denial'

The subtleties and paradoxes of communicating with the patient with cancer cannot be understood — and his fears cannot be handled sympathetically — without some insight into the gradient formed by varying degrees of hope, optimism, and denial. Each may be slight or considerable and, as in normal life, may vary from day to day and from month to month. 'Denial' (not a very satisfactory word, but the best we have) is when a person takes a less serious view of what is happening to him than he would do if it was happening to somebody else; 'forgets' what he has been told about his diagnosis or prognosis; or 'denies' some unpleasant possibility. Opinions will always differ as to how common this is. It depends on whether slight denial, perhaps affecting only some of the more unpleasant possibilities, is included or not. Failure to recognise denial may lead to costly mistakes, with needless damage to morale. Some patients can accept blunt talk about a bad prognosis, provided they have 'not got cancer'. Others are exactly the opposite. They can accept that they have a kind of cancer, but cannot tolerate a bad prognosis. Thus diagnosis may be denied and prognosis accepted or vice versa.

The doctor needs to be sensitive to such alternatives and to conflicts in a patient's mind arising from occasional or sustained use of this useful, perhaps essential, protective mechanism, which may be quite fragile (easily upset by a chance remark; a newspaper article about cancer; the death of another patient) or more deep seated. Sometimes a patient 'knows' and sometimes he does not. Perhaps when he is with one person he seems to know; when he is with another he seems not to know; He may know; but not want to think about it. His mood changes. Perhaps he accepts probable death, but can still plan for possible recovery or remission. "He may suspect," wrote Barber, "that he is just building castles in the air — and why not — to some extent he has done it all his life"[6]. He may have no illusions, but not want to talk about it. We all know how much it can hurt to have something said aloud that we have suspected for some time. Something that we know deep down, but not superficially — in other words we show a degree of denial. Finally, a patient may show denial to such an extent that friends and relatives can scarcely credit it; and those looking after him, perhaps unwilling to accept the concept of denial, may attribute such 'lack of insight' to brain metastases.

Hospital staff sometimes say about a patient, "he is not stupid, he must know the score perfectly well". But denial is not related to intelligence. Nor to knowledge; it is quite common in doctors who develop cancer. In some ways it can be thought of as the opposite to excessive anxiety — for example, fear of flying, perhaps following some frightening incident. Such fears have little to do with knowledge or intelligence. The ambivalent feelings we all have about these things are shown clearly when on the one hand we talk of 'wishful thinking' or 'self-deception', as if this were always unhealthy or a sign of a weak character; and when on the other hand we admire optimism and 'refusal to accept defeat' (often associated with a contempt for pessimistic statistics and gloomy expert opinions) as a sign of strength, resilience, and courage. It has been said that denial in serious illness is just as common, perhaps even more common, in those with a strong personality who have led successful lives.

Optimism or 'acceptance'?

We may feel more humble and better able to understand the optimism and denial of some of our patients (and their doubts about the wisdom of asking for more information[5,7-9]) if we reflect on the situation that we all face in the last quarter of the twentieth century. Suppose we are asked to say — publicly or in the presence of younger members of our family — what we believe to be the prognosis of our society. Would we describe the chances of dying within the next 20 years from violence (nuclear or otherwise) as (a) very small; (b) appreciable; or (c) more likely than not? The question is a fair one, objective and dispassionate, but we are quite likely to be annoyed by it and to refuse to take it seriously, a sure sign that to do so might disturb our protective defence mechanisms, or those of others (whom we do not wish to hurt). If we are asked about some even more unpleasant possibility, such as hunger or starvation, our unwillingness to discuss the matter will be even greater, although observers from another planet would see nothing fanciful in such a question. Like our patients with cancer who fear possible recurrence and death, we are likely to feel that since there is little we can do about it, and since it may never happen, it is foolish to dwell on the matter and pointless to ask for more information. Much better to get on with living our lives and forget about it.

If a patient soon denies what he has been told[10], does this mean that it would have been better to handle his case differently? I think it often does. A period of shock and depression, followed by denial because what has been said is intolerable, means a period of unnecessary distress that could have been avoided. Nobody has benefited. Either the patient has been wrongly assessed, or his peace of mind has been deliberately sacrificed, perhaps in the name of some over-rigid dogma or rule of thumb, based on the idea of 'always being honest'; perhaps with the hope of ultimately reducing public fear of certain words; perhaps for real or imagined medicolegal reasons. Much has been written about patients moving gradually from denial towards 'acceptance', but it is also quite common to see a change in the opposite direction, from acceptance to denial; and this may be seen both in those doing badly and in those doing well. The idea that acceptance is inherently preferable to denial and that this should always be the ultimate, if not the immediate aim, is too doctrinaire. It is usually wiser not to try too hard to alter these things. Limited explanations, which might seem lame and incomplete if denial were absent, can bring valuable comfort and encouragement when it is present.

When it occurs, sustained absence of denial is impressive. "*Aren't I lucky to have such beautiful weather for my last summer?*" was the consistent, calm mood of one recent patient, a 50-year-old unmarried teacher, who said she had no religious faith. But this is not common. Similarly, situations where husband and wife both accept and discuss freely with each other (and perhaps even with their friends) the expected forthcoming death of one of them can occasionally work well and be touching and ennobling. But, once again, such an approach for months on end seems to suit only a few. Attempts to achieve such acceptance in unsuitable cases can damage the relationship between doctor and patient and lead to considerable distress, at least until a measure of hope and denial reassert themselves and mercifully heal the pain and feeling of hopelessness that had become insupportable. Even in dying patients, Hinton[11] found complete acceptance in only five out of 60 of those he interviewed.

The evidence of certain kinds of inquiry (for example, asking healthy people if they would like to be told if they were dying; or asking patients with cancer if they approve of having been told the full facts) needs to be treated with the greatest reserve. Understandable pride, self respect, and concern not to seem cowardly are likely to distort the findings to such an extent that such studies cannot be taken at their face value. Of more interest is the fact that when the bereaved relatives of 785 patients were interviewed by independent observers[12], only 2% definitely considered that it would have been better if those who did not appear to know the probable outcome of their illness had known. Elizabeth Kubler-Ross[13] in her carefully detailed and sensitive study of dying patients goes so far as to say that "*even the most accepting, the most realistic patient, left the possibility open for some cure . . . they showed the greatest confidence in the doctors who allowed for such hope — realistic or not — and appreciated it when hope was offered in spite of bad news*".

Diagnosis

Most of us like to think of ourselves as robust personalities, calling a spade a spade, not afraid to tell the truth, however unpalatable, and not afraid to hear it. The doctor wants to have a reputation for speaking fully and frankly. The man in the street likes to feel that if he ever had cancer he would welcome this approach. The reality is rather different. Sometimes blunt talk is refreshing and valuable. But at other times to be silent about all or part of the truth is essential if we are not to cause pointless distress. To be considerate is to be discreet. Euphemisms are a part of life, and of good manners, and plain language may often be offensive. Most of us enjoy eating the flesh of dead animals and drinking their blood, so long as both are cooked first. But we do not express it like this to our host or hostess.

It is often the same with the word 'cancer'. Taboos and attitudes change. Discussion is less inhibited than it was 20 years ago. But there are still a lot of patients in every walk of life (and probably in every country) who cannot cope emotionally with 'having cancer' in the way that they cope with having, say, heart disease of roughly equivalent seriousness. For them it is a cruel and painful word, suggesting a horrible unclean disease ("we don't know the cause, it could happen to anyone" is often useful reassurance), probably incurable and certainly incompatible with a normal life unless speedily and totally eradicated. Immediate use of the word cancer is to some (not all) patients as unfortunate as bluntly telling others that they have epilepsy, or schizophrenia, or that they will be crippled for life, when they are quite unprepared for such harsh, blunt words.

It is revealing that even doctors who are most anxious to use the word cancer initially in the interest of 'complete honesty', will seldom use it subsequently, unless the patient particularly seems to want this, which few do. Such a doctor is no more likely to ask, "how is the cancer getting on?" than is his colleague who has avoided using the word from the start. Many patients find that if they use the word too freely their friends are embarrassed and avoid them. MacIntosh[7] observed during prolonged observation of patients with cancer in hospital that most of those who 'knew' or 'probably knew' preferred to use euphemisms when talking to each other. To complicate matters further, when we speak of 'having cancer', 'having a curable kind of cancer', 'having a small tumour', or 'having a growth', there are subtle overtones which may make one phrase much less frightening than another, although all may be true. Because of this, and because of varying degrees of denial, the very same phrases that insult the dignity and intelligence of one patient (he would prefer blunter language) may bring valuable comfort and encouragement to another.

Again, suppose a patient with a cancer that carries a good chance of cure — a small early malignant melanoma perhaps, or a carcinoma confined to the cervix — asks if she has 'got cancer'. The problem now may be not so much 'should the truth be told', but what exactly is 'the truth'? If this patient is terrified, having firmly believed all her life that to have 'cancer' is to have a widespread disease, shameful and hopeless, it is usually just wishful thinking for the doctor to imagine that he can eradicate at a stroke the convictions of a lifetime by giving a brief enlightened account of the facts. It follows that it may be true and not false to assure the patient (speaking to her in her language, not ours) that she does not have cancer, but that we advise thorough radiotherapy or surgery (as the case may be) as a precaution — an insurance policy, if you like, for the future.

When we talk of 'the truth', we have to think of the likely effect on the hearer. The ill-advised use of blunt 'honest' language may easily leave the patient with an unshakable and untrue conviction that his condition is much worse than it really is.

Prognosis

Patients with cancer are generally considered to have a very good prognosis if, for example, 80% of a group can expect to be alive and well in 10 years; and as having a very poor prognosis if only 20% can hope for this. But there is another way of looking at such figures. In both these situations the pessimist may be justifiably gloomy about the very real possibility of his cancer proving fatal. The optimist, however, with equal justification, may be encouraged by the very real possibility of being alive and well in 10 years time. Similarly, if 95% of patients are likely to die from a particular kind of cancer the doctor may feel that it might just as well be 100%; but the two situations are very different to the patient who longs for reassurance that his outlook is not hopeless. Especially if he is told (truthfully and emphatically) that there is no reason why he should not be one of the lucky ones who has no further trouble. Acceptance of the possibility of life soon coming to an end is very common, especially in the elderly. But living with a certain 'death sentence' seems to be intolerable to most people, except for fairly short periods (a month or so at most).

How small does a hope of cure have to be before it is called a false hope? There is no answer to this. Nevertheless, the popular idea that optimism concerning cancer is always less truthful than pessimism must be firmly rejected. The hard evidence of cancer statistics allows far more than a grain of hope to many with a serious outlook and often justifies restrained, responsible optimism ('*potentially very serious, but certainly far from hopeless*', for example) — a very different thing to the pretence and insincerity of false optimism. It also helps to remind many patients, especially if they are over 60, that it is absurd to divide all people of their age into those with a terrible question mark hanging over them (because of some medical condition that might recur) and those with a guaranteed future. For several reasons, the latter idea is clearly a myth, for no such group exists: to some extent we are all in the same boat, patients or not. A distinct rise in the morale of a ward of male patients with cancer was noted by our nursing staff in Glasgow at the time of the tragic Ibrox football stadium disaster in which 66 Glasgow football fans died.

If things look really bad, and it seems right to tell the patient so, many studies have emphasised that much will depend on how this is done, including not only the choice of words, but the warmth or coldness of the doctor's manner and many other subtle and intangible factors. Because patients vary, the very same words spoken in the same way by the same doctor can be completely right for one patient and quite wrong for another. Because doctors and nurses vary, the phrases that suit the personality of one are quite unsuitable for use by another. This is not just a medical matter. It is part of leadership and life in general. In 1940 Winston Churchill began one of his wartime radio talks to the British people with the simple, emphatic, and incredibly blunt words: "*The news from France is very bad.*" Yet because of the way he said it and because of his personality, the morale of those of us who heard him rose rather than fell, and confidence in him (and in ourselves) grew before he had said another word.

Although in some ways such situations differ from that of advanced cancer, it seems to help medical students, young nurses, and trainee social workers (some of whom feel that it must surely be the doctor's duty to tell every patient the full facts) if we discuss with them problems of leadership and morale in a non-medical context. Suppose a plane crashes in an isolated area where the chance of ever being found is remote and where every aspect of the situation is as bad as it can be. The 'honest' leader, who considers that every survivor, whatever his age or condition, has a right to know that there is '*no hope*' (and who advises acceptance of a slow and certain death, rather than 'pretending' otherwise) will not be very popular. Few will have any confidence in him. Morale will suffer. Many will want to choose a new leader. Equally unfortunate for most people would be the leader who, hoping to improve morale in the short term, uses false optimism to pretend that the situation is not serious. Often the best leader is the one with the strength of character to keep his worst fears to himself and who says, "*We are in a very tough spot, there is no doubt about that; I can promise nothing, but I think we have a chance, in fact, I know we have,*" and who then outlines a plan of action, calculated to take full advantage of whatever small chance exists.

Avoiding extremes

Between the extremes of cold or excessively pessimistic 'honesty' on the one hand, and what is sometimes called the 'pathetic charade' of deception on the other, lies a complex range of various more civilised and generally preferable options. Some are a blend of bluntness and cautious optimism. Some are based on talking to the patient in such a way that he is, in effect, given the choice of either denial or acceptance. Some depend on unspoken communication, many patients preferring to be *'told'* in this way, rather than to have everything spelt out to them. Some rest on the fact that, although many patients are grateful to have someone looking after them who is not afraid to discuss cancer, death, and dying, many others prefer their doctor to talk about something more cheerful.

Each option, whether applied to diagnosis or to prognosis, is infinitely flexible. As doctors, concerned only with doing our best for each patient, we should take full advantage of this fact. To do so need not in any way compromise our integrity. It is sometimes wise to be much more blunt about diagnosis than about prognosis; and sometimes vice versa. With some patients optimism carries more conviction when salted with some unpalatable facts and possibilities. With others, especially if they are frail and elderly, to do this, or even to hint at percentages and survival statistics is clumsy and thoughtless. Some patients, for various reasons including old age, deafness, and extreme anxiety, are especially prone to misinterpret or misquote what we say. When we talk to them it may well be that the fewer words we use and the simpler our message the better, otherwise what we say may increase rather than decrease their doubts and fears.

It may seem unduly paternalistic, even arrogant, to make arbitrary decisions of this kind, calculated to emphasise the more hopeful aspects of a situation or to protect the patient from the full rigours of *'the truth'*. But are we not being at least equally 'arrogant' if we insist, often to the dismay of the relatives, that we have a duty to be blunt and to give full information, whether the patient seems to want this or not? What right have we, if the outlook is bleak, to conceal elements of doubt about the diagnosis, extent of spread, or prognosis, on the grounds that to speak of them might *'raise false hopes'*? It can be very encouraging for a patient to be told that there are few certainties in medicine. Is it not inevitable that we are selective and arbitrary to some extent, not only in our choice of words, but in emphasis and manner? Have we the right in a serious situation to do what Oliver Wendell Holmes[14] called *"cheating the patient out of his natural birthright of hope of recovery"*? Since we cannot be entirely sure what is going to happen in any individual case, an impression that we have not given up hope is usually preferable to an impression that we have — at least until it is clearly peace and an end to striving, rather than **'hope'**, that the patient and relatives long for.

Slogans and catch-phrases do not solve these sensitive problems. If euphemisms are to be banned as dishonest, or criticised as perpetuating the fear of certain words, and if the doctor has a duty always to tell the whole truth, it is not only patients with cancer who will suffer. What of the patient who asks "*I am not going mad, am I?*" What if the prognosis is so bad that the only 'honest' reply to this question (avoiding all euphemism and pretence, so that the patient has confidence in us and can see that we are not afraid of the word '*mad*') is "*I'm afraid you probably are*"?

Interprofessional communication

Few patients suffer a sharper drop in morale than those transferred from one doctor or one medical team to another, who get the impression that little or no information has been passed on. Consistently efficient and immediate interprofessional communication, so hard to achieve in practice, should not only be good, but be seen by the patient to be good, and he should be specifically reassured on this point. At first sight it might be desirable that such information should always include a note about what the patient knows or has been told about diagnosis or prognosis. There are certainly occasions when this is appropriate and helpful. Yet many doctors, though sensitive to the problem, seldom mention it, even in a lengthy exchange of information. Why is this? Firstly, because they have probably avoided the extremes already mentioned, and no simple statement can convey all the subtleties of emphasis, choice of words, optimism, and patient reaction that have occurred (perhaps on more than one occasion and with more than one member of staff). The inevitable gross over-simplification can be very misleading. Secondly, the patient's mood and the varying proportions of acceptance, denial, optimism, and pessimism that contribute to it, remain fluid. Each new doctor or member of staff has to assess the current situation for himself. To try to describe what has already passed between patient and staff (unless something striking or unusual has happened) may only encourage an undesirably rigid idea that the problem has been dealt with.

Medical social workers and others, seeing a patient for the first time after being informed that he knows his diagnosis and prognosis, are often puzzled to find that this does not appear to be the case. The cause is twofold. Firstly, when doctors talk of '*telling*' or '*not telling*' the patient, they differ considerably as to what they mean by these phrases. Many British doctors, for example, believe that in the United States "*they tell all their patients*". Yet it was recently claimed in an American medical journal that 90% of American doctors '*usually do not tell*'[15]. Secondly, the denial mechanism and a preference for euphemisms may have already come into play, and perhaps the patient totally suppresses part of what was said to him and emphasises another part.

Sometimes it is suggested that the best solution to this problem is to leave all such discussion to the family doctor, who probably knows the patient, his family, and his responsibilities better. But there are serious objections to this. Firstly, the specialist has first-hand knowledge of all the benefits and side-effects experienced by many other patients in a similar situation. The patient senses this and realises that he is not just getting a second-hand opinion or a view based on a fairly small experience of his particular problem. Secondly, to delay until the patient sees his own doctor can cause unacceptable anxiety. Thirdly, the hospital doctor, particularly if he specialises in cancer, has a far better chance than the family doctor of being able to provide valuable encouragement by telling of a similar patient who responded well to treatment; perhaps of one who recently attended for a checkup, who is back at work and enjoying life. A specialist in a large centre, unlike the family doctor, may refer to such cases without risk of breach of confidence.

Conclusion

"It is fear that I stand most in fear of," wrote Montaigne nearly 400 years ago, *"in sharpness it exceeds every other feeling".* So we must try to relieve this particular form of suffering, just as we try to relieve pain; and good communication can often do this better than any drug. We must communicate both efficiency and kindness; and we must not confuse diagnosis with prognosis. Whatever the outlook, our main objective is to maintain morale and to help the patient to achieve maximum courage, equanimity, and peace of mind, but not in a shortsighted way which will create difficulties later on. Most of us prefer to be pragmatic, in the best sense of the word, rather than to follow some set dogma; to assess as best we can (preferably with the help of relatives and nursing staff) the immediate and late effects of what we have said or not said, modifying accordingly our future policy in similar circumstances; and trying to learn from our mistakes, just as we do in any other aspect of patient care.

Central to the art of good communication is firstly to try to get the amount of information and explanation about right. Lack of information can greatly increase anxiety and stress (knowledge is the antidote to fear, said Emerson) — but so can too much of it. Secondly, whether the outlook is good or bad, to give appropriate reassurance and encouragement. There is always something to reassure the patient about and nearly always something to be positive and optimistic about, even if this is only the prospect of symptom relief. Thirdly, to be watchful and flexible, especially if there is a change (as there often is) either in the prognosis, in the patient's attitude, or in his threshold for anxiety and depression. And finally — sometimes directly in serious conversation, sometimes indirectly, by word or by manner, by humour or by friendship — to remind the patient whose outlook is serious, but not hopeless, that few things in this world are certain and that the difference between the uncertainties that he faces and those faced by others his age may be only a matter of degree. We are all travelling the same road.

References

1. Saunders, C M, in *Scientific Foundations of Oncology*, ed T Symington, p 673. London, Heinemann, 1976.

2. Brewin, T B, in *Cancer Priorities*. London, British Cancer Council, 1971.

3. Hutchison, R, *British Medical Journal*, 1928, 1, 335.

4. Abrams, R, *New England Journal of Medicine*, 1966, **274**, 317.

5. Aldrich, C K, *Journal of the American Medical Association,* 1963, **184**, 329.

6. Barber, H, *The Practitioner*, 1948, **161**, 76.

7. McIntosh, J, *Lancet*, 1976, **2**, 300.

8. Chesser, E S, and Anderson, J L, *Proceedings of the Royal Society of Medicine*, 1975, **68**, 793.

9. Witzel, L, *British Medical Journal*, 1975, **2**, 81.

10. Aitken-Swan, J and Easson, E C, *British Medical Journal*, 1959, **1**, 779.

11. Hinton, J, *British Medical Journal*, 1974, **3**, 25.

12. Cartwright, A, Hockey, L, and Anderson, J L, *Life Before Death*. London, Routledge and Kegan Paul, 1973.

13. Kubler-Ross, E, *On Death and Dying*. London, Tavistock Publications, 1970.

14. Holmes, O W, *The Professor at the Breakfast Table*. Boston, 1859.

15. Schneiderman, L J, *New England Journal of Medicine*, 1977, **216**, 825.

Three ways of giving bad news

Reprinted from
The Lancet, 1991, Vol 337, pages 1207–1209

When patients complain about how they were given bad news they may have good cause. Or it may be that they are just raging at fate and feel like shooting the messenger. Either way their distress might have been less if the situation had been handled more sensitively. Here is a personal view, concerned not with the eternal dilemmas of whether and when to give bad news but with how it is done, once the decision to do it has been taken.

The three ways

The first way of giving bad news (the 'three ways' suggested here are, of course, crude simplifications) is the blunt and unfeeling way. Perhaps the doctor just stands at the foot of the bed in a white coat, looking down at the patient. The excuse is that the patient will inevitably be upset and that little can be done about it.

The second way—let's call it the kind and sad way—is to be private, concerned, and unhurried, but to regard the matter as just a painful duty. The bad news is given gravely and solemnly, with little positive support or encouragement. Sympathy and compassion are fine qualities, but an excess of them can lower morale. There is also a danger that the patient, not listening properly to what is said and judging mainly from the doctor's manner, thinks the position is worse than it is. Another common feature is that what was decided beforehand is said in full, without modification, either because the doctor thinks that to modify it would be wrong or because he or she is too unhappy and ill at ease to look the patient in the eye — so there is little or no feedback. Typically, there is also a fear of raising false hopes. Encouraging possibilities are not mentioned. The doctor may feel that in a serious situation optimism is short-sighted and also perhaps the mark of the charlatan. This stance is based partly on what is thought to be in the patient's best interest. But it is also a form of defensive medicine. The idea is that even a chink of hope increases the risk of criticism (or worse still of litigation) should things go badly. Finally, it is feared that anything beyond the plain facts may invite the currently dreaded accusation of 'paternalism'.

The third way I shall call the understanding and positive way. Its essential ingredients are: flexibility, based on feedback, while giving the bad news; and positive thinking, reassurance, and planning for the immediate future, all blended with the bad news, not just saved for later.

More subtle and sensitive than the second way, this third way needs a light touch, together with something intangible that, if we could identify it, ought to help a young person to get into medical school. And it need not take any longer, expecially since periods of sad silence are often a feature of the second way. It's quality, not quantity, that counts.

Feedback

It helps if something is already known of the foibles, strengths, and weaknesses of the patient. But, even then, assessment throughout the interview is vital for deciding what to say next; which words to use; which not to use; and what to emphasise. To the sensitive observer, the patient's face will usually show quite clearly whether what has just been said and how it was said have helped comprehension and morale (in which case it should be reinforced) or not (in which case another approach should be tried). If the doctor is to be understanding and on the same wavelength as the patient, communication must be two way. Those who are uneasy about doctors' modifying their conversation with patients in this way forget that this is only what considerate people do when speaking to their friends in everyday life, especially in a crisis.

Another thing that should be fairly easy to spot is the glazed look that means the patient is no longer listening. If in doubt, tactfully check: "*Many people say that after being given bad news they hardly heard another word. I'd probably be the same myself. How about you? What was the last thing you heard me say?*" If necessary, stop and arrange a second interview, which can sometimes be carried out in a friendly and surprisingly satisfactory way over the phone.

A second kind of feedback is equally valuable. To make a better job of talking to this patient in the future (and to learn from our mistakes so that we do better with others) our own assessment may not be enough. The doctor must also take every opportunity to find out from nurses or relatives the effect of what was said on the patient's understanding and morale. It may be that the bad news was interpreted in too optimistic or too pessimistic a way; that a phrase used had an unduly depressing or frightening effect; that there has been a misunderstanding that needs to be put right; that too much was said and the patient is confused; or not enough, so that he or she fears something is being concealed.

Examples of the third way

Among the myriad ways of giving bad news, here are some examples of being truthful yet positive. They are just suggestions, based on the kind of feedback just described. Some help some patients, some help others. Some suit some doctors better than others. And there must be real sincerity, not some stale formula. Sudden impulses as to what to say can be quite inspired; but inevitably some doctors and nurses have a better feel for this sort of thing than others.

Various current jokes about 'the good news and the bad news' may mean it is better to avoid these precise phrases. Nevertheless, any 'good news' (bolstered by warm emphasis rather than offered in a cold, halfhearted way as a small crumb of comfort) can be an ally in the fight against low morale. "I'm afraid the tests show...", then continuing with emphasis and without any pause after giving the bad news, "but I'm glad to say that the position is at least more hopeful than some cases we see", or, "at least the liver seems normal and healthy, which is a relief". Positive words and statements (such as "normal and healthy") are usually preferable to negative ones (such as "not involved" or, worse still, the medical jargon that says "your scan is negative").

"At least we now know exactly what we are up against and what has to be done (or what the options are)" often helps. Even if it is just symptom relief and help with daily living, there must be a plan, and a promise that there will always be other things that can be tried, and an understanding that the doctor will never lose interest in the patient's progress, whether or not directly concerned in his or her care.

Nothing in medicine is certain. "Statistically it looks bad. You wouldn't get a life insurance company to give you cover; at least not at normal rates. But then *they are a mean lot, aren't they? They are not interested in the way in which some people, against all the odds, do amazingly well".*

Mention a patient who did well. For many people, one seems to be just as encouraging as more than one. And everything said must be true. *"Yesterday I saw a man who two years ago had a similar outlook to the one you have now. He is at work and enjoying life and has just got back suntanned after a holiday in Spain".* Note that this other patient need not have had the same disease, so long as the prognosis was roughly the same. For example, 5 and 10 year survival figures for several common cancer situations are very similar to those for some of the commonest cardiovascular disorders.

Some patients feel better if reminded of the terrible uncertainty faced by so-called normal, healthy people, any of whom could be killed in a road accident or die from a sudden heart attack. A variation on this theme (especially useful for elderly people with cancer of average prognosis) is to say with mock seriousness, *"Put it like this, it's quite possible that the next time you are in hospital it will be for something different".* Which at first sight doesn't sound very friendly or encouraging. Nor would it be, if said in the wrong way, or to the wrong patient, or at the wrong moment. But when it fits, when it is on target, it is the sort of thing that can take the sharp edge off the bad news; help towards a more philosophical attitude to sudden misfortune; and bring closer together 'victims' of one kind or another and 'normal' people of the same age.

Mention that research is going an all the time (*"you never know—a new treatment could be discovered"*). And sometimes, very gently and tactfully, steer the patient towards a little counting of blessings.

Hope and empathy

The first thing that is said is often remembered best; and may even be the only thing retained. Forget the medical routine that always gives the diagnosis first. Vary it a bit. Sometimes give the plan for the immediate future first, before the bad news. Or sometimes say at the beginning, *"Now, the first thing I want to stress is this. Whatever I tell you in a moment about exactly what we have found and so on, I want you to promise me that you will hang on to this fact: the situation is serious, but far from hopeless, you have a chance of doing well."*

The exact words used will depend both on the prognosis and on the fact that some people need more optimism than others. Not foolish promises, but sincere controlled optimism. Then if things go badly, doctor and patient share disappointment just as they previously shared hope, and their relationship is unharmed.

There is also a limit to how much bad news some people can take, at least at one interview. And a few prefer pessimism — perhaps, to heighten the drama and give the best possible chance of later proving the doctor wrong.

Reassurance is perfectly consistent with bad news. No matter what the outlook, some of the patient's fears will be needless. Two points about the art of reassurance are especially relevant. Mention of something that the patient was not worrying about is not only unnecessary, it can create new anxieties. And indirect reassurance is usually more effective than direct. "What will you do for your holiday next year if you are fit enough?" is helpful to the person who had given up hope of ever having a holiday again.

Emphasising the extent or severity of the problem, the opposite to what reassures most patients, can help others. Some are relieved to learn that they have not been making a fuss, that their symptoms have been fully justified. And some love a bit of melodrama, especially if linked to the breaking of some local record — the biggest tumour seen on the ward so far this year, or the second worst heart attack, or the most blood lost. These are useful consolations for the hardship and heartache of being ill. Something, perhaps, to tell friends and neighbours. But be sure to choose the right patient.

The place of irrelevant small talk, usually at the end of the interview and said almost as if no bad news had ever been given, is interesting. Anyone who thinks that this must be in bad taste is making a mistake. Feedback shows that it can help to combat fear and a feeling of depression and hopelessness. But be careful. The ice is sometimes thin.

Unspoken communication is probably at least as important as what is said. The doctor must not look or sound frightened. It helps if he or she has a quiet, yet strong and confident personality while being natural, warm, and friendly. To this end always sit down with the patient; and, though it may seem absurd to specify this, doctor and patient are usually best neither facing each other, nor sitting side by side, but at about ninety degrees. They should also be within reach, so that each can touch the other, either when seeking comfort or when giving it. By touch I am thinking mainly of a spontaneous grip of the hand; but any other accessible spot, proximal or distal, will do.

The doctor must seem to the patient to have at least some idea of what it's like to be on the receiving end. To put it bluntly — to know what hell it can be. He or she must show warmth, understanding, and empathy. These feelings probably come across better when they are transmitted in an unspoken rather than a spoken way. For example, a smile of the right kind can carry powerful messages that have nothing to do with humour. Strange as it may seem I would say that in almost any interview that gives bad news there should be at least a glimmer of a smile at some stage. It is difficult to be really supportive and friendly without it — a sincere, affectionate, and understanding smile, probably expressed as much in the eyes as in the mouth. But can such things ever be taught? God forbid that any medical student should be told to practise in front of a mirror.

Probably there is nothing new in all this. I would guess that ten thousand years ago there were some witch doctors giving bad news the first way, some the second way, and some the third way. The third way is more flexible than the second way. It need not be shortsighted. It takes more account of the varying reactions, hopes, and fears of each patient, helping each to cope in his or her own way. It is more positive, blending reassurance and encouragement with the bad news. Shock is reduced. Anger is less likely. And it's not so sad.

———————

Not that it's easy to strike a balance between hope and gloom. It isn't. Hang ups and misconceptions about cancer lie deeply embedded in the human psyche and it's hard to shift them. But take, for example, the situation — so common in breast, prostate, or colorectal cancer — when nobody knows for sure if cure has been achieved or not. Might it not sometimes be better, at least with older patients, to do more to encourage the sort of philosophical outlook seen in those of their own age with heart problems. They, too, have to live with the possibility of recurrence at any time. They, too, don't know (any more than any of us do) when or how they will finally die. The important thing is that whether ex-cardiac or ex-cancer — and whether cured or not — all have a chance of living full and happy lives for many years.

(Extract from a book review, *Brit Med J* 1993 **307** 75)

Truth, trust, and paternalism

Reprinted from
The Lancet,
1985, Vol ii, pages 490–492

Let's be a little more honest about the importance of 'being honest'. We need to strike a balance between 'informed consent' and 'paternalism'. The idea of the first as a great good and the second as a great evil is today in danger of being carried to absurd lengths. Yet few doctors dare say so (at any rate in public) for fear of being called paternalistic, old fashioned, arrogant — or worse.

Communication is of crucial importance in medicine. Partly to inform, explain, and advise. And partly — especially when a patient is frightened, ill, weak, or otherwise vulnerable — to raise morale, give confidence, encourage, and protect. Whether or not we call this 'paternalism', the fact is that to try and abolish it would be a sure way to add greatly to the sum total of human suffering.

Unfortunately, as so often in life, one aim may conflict with the other. To compromise makes us feel uncomfortable. We would prefer to be guided by some noble moral principle. But such principles — pure and inspiring though they seem at first sight — are liable to give contradictory advice. Sanctity of life is a precious concept, but most people feel that it has to be restrained at times, if it is not to cause excessive suffering or distress. The rights of the individual may have to be curtailed in the interests of the community. Similarly, though we all prize truthfulness, there are times when the thought of *'telling someone the truth'* — or a particular part of it — may seem so cruel and pointless that most of us (whether doctors or not) will decide against it.

It is easy to denigrate compromise of this kind. But sometimes the only alternative is to embrace one noble principle and murder another. Which seems even worse. So we compromise; but, we hope, in a civilised and humane manner.

Two new books provide good examples of the tendency to stress the first aim of communication at the expense of the second. One, written jointly by a journalist and a doctor[1], covers all kinds of ethical dilemma (abortion, embryo research, confidentiality, resource allocation, and so on) and is recommended for the fair and thorough way it deals with most of them. However, when it comes to 'informed consent' both this book and the other (written by a journalist on her own[2]) give views which, I would guess, will be judged by future generations to be lacking in balance. The advantages of trying to explain risks and options to all patients are well set out, but the serious limitations and disadvantages are too often played down or ignored.

Here are two uncompromising extracts from the first book[1]:

Page 144: *"Consent is meaningless unless it is informed. And it is not possible for the patient to be informed unless he has been told the whole truth about himself".*

Page 173: *"The patient's most important safeguard is for the doctor to tell the truth — not simply never to lie, but not to withhold information... for without information there can be no consent to treatment".*

This sort of thing sounds fine until we come down to earth and think it through, in terms of practical everyday life. Is consent really to be judged *"meaningless unless it is informed"*? What about trust? If I seek the help of an accountant, builder, lawyer, or cobbler, my consent to what he does with my money, my house, my reputation, or my shoes is likely to be based on a blend of information and trust. Of course, I may want to discuss certain options and risks. But the more trust the less need for me to ask a lot of searching questions. Thus saving both his time and mine.

As soon as the expert that I consult sees what the problem is, may I not just trust him to do his best and get on with it? Does he have to keep explaining to every client or customer why he prefers his own particular way of doing things? Or how he has been lately trying out new methods? Or how somebody in a similar situation once finished up worse off instead of better off? And if he 'deliberately conceals' such things (partly because if he tried to explain everything to everybody he could never get on with his work) is he being unethical? Is his failure to tell the whole truth to be judged morally equivalent to telling a lie?

What happens when the element of fear is injected into a non-medical situation? Most people facing death or danger during a hijack, the failure of an aircraft, or some other disaster will feel safer if there is some leadership. A good leader behaves in a very similar way to a good doctor in a medical crisis[3]. Much will depend on his personality, but he must not be too optimistic, nor too pessimistic. He must be blunt enough to get everyone's confidence, but he will often keep to himself certain grim possibilities and certain areas of doubt or confusion. Nearly everyone will see this as part of his job and will not think any less of him for it. Nobody calls him a paternalist just because he uses his discretion. Words of encouragement that cut no ice with people who are not unduly frightened may greatly help those who are. If he does a good job he can improve morale immeasurably. Above all, he does not just blindly dish out 'complete honesty' and tell everybody everything that they 'have a right to know'. It is not that easy. Nor will he — if he has a grain of sense — ask each person to choose if they want to know the full facts or not. What are they supposed to say? And what will be the subsequent state of mind of someone who replies that he prefers not to know? Will he not just feel a coward and worry about what others have been told?

Moreover, trust is a marvellous time saver. Whether we are speaking of medical or non-medical problems, discussions of risks and options may, of course, have a high priority. On the other hand, it does not make sense to allow lengthy low-priority explanations to encroach too far into available time, leading to less work done and fewer people helped. How strange that this obvious and important point regarding priorities is so seldom mentioned by those who urge patients and others not to take so much on trust. They seem to imagine that vast chunks of time can be plucked out of thin air without any damage to general standards of care and efficiency.

Trust also means less risk of those misconceptions that experience teaches us can arise so easily when detailed information is given. Phillips and Dawson, the authors of the first book I am quoting, believe that *"to argue that detail equals confusion is an example of the worst kind of paternalism"*. But any doctor who asks a patient or relative at the end of a lengthy interview (or even a brief one) *"what will you say if someone asks you what I have told you?"*, soon discovers how common are immediate misconceptions — quite apart from how much is remembered later. Evidence confirms it[4]. And this is hardly surprising. Picture a doctor in his own home discussing complicated matters with his plumber. How will he get on if he tries to repeat it all to a friend a week later? And supposing experience has taught the plumber that, although some doctors understand what he is talking about, others don't — and suppose that the plumber (especially when he is busy) says to the customer "*you will just have to trust me to do the best job I can*". Is that arrogant paternalism?

True, there are patients getting too much paternalism and not enough explanation. But when it is the other way round it is much less likely to be reported. No patient is going to complain that he was told too much. Nor that when he was frightened nobody held his hand.

Fortunately for general standards of medical care, a fair amount of trust and a limited amount of information about risks and options still suits many patients very well (including many doctors when they are ill)—at least in the United Kingdom. Others (again including many doctors, who vary just as much as anyone else) prefer a lot of information and are greatly reassured by it. Knowledge can improve morale. So can trust. Sometimes it is right to discuss painful choices with the patient, even though they will distress him. Sometimes it seems better not to. As in ordinary life, only a very insensitive person believes that what is best for one patient is necessarily best for another. Moreover, the very same person may need much more protection (paternalism if you like) at one stage of his illness than at another[3].

Such a regard for individual variations seems to worry some anti-paternalists almost more than consistent paternalism. All patients should be treated alike, they seem to say. Not to do so is arrogant.

Also very common is a remarkable ambivalence towards this question of whether or not the doctor should use his discretion. Here are some examples from the second book (Faulder[2]). On the one hand we are told that "*The medical consensus…is that remote risks do not need to be revealed… the patient will be told only what the doctors think it is fit for her to know…this outrageous paternalism has been endorsed in case after case in the English courts*". And that, "*Either a moral right [the right to informed consent] exists or it does not. If it does, then it is universal and no-one has the right to deny it to anyone*". Also that, "*Informed consent…is neither a concession nor a courtesy to be granted by well disposed doctors as and when they see fit, but an inalienable human right…*". Yet on other pages we read that "*A doctor has to tread very carefully. Some information he must volunteer, but if he sees that the patient is shutting herself off from hearing too much, although agreeing to his proposals for treatment, then he is justified in presuming that she is giving her consent… this kind of signalling from the patient is usually expressed tacitly*". And elsewhere that "*It is equally a denial of autonomy to force unwanted information on those* *who have clearly indicated, **not necessarily verbally***" [my emphasis] "*that they do not want it*". We also read that, "*Doctors argue with some truth that it is all very well for the strong and healthy to cry shame, but paternalism is still what the vast majority of their patients thrust upon them*". And that "*It is far too easy for the outsider to condemn doctors for not telling the truth*".

Phillips and Dawson[1] would presumably disagree with this last comment. "*We feel*", they say, "*that the importance of telling the truth cannot be over-estimated*". But, like many other fine principles, we all know in our heart of hearts that this is not so. It *can* be overestimated. Easily. 'Truth', in fact, can sometimes create havoc. One distinguished American journalist learnt this during his own illness and was not afraid to say so afterwards. "*Most doctors*", he said, "*are panic producers without realising it... they underestimate the extent to which their truths become death sentences*"[5].

Many friends and relatives curse the clumsy insensitivity of doctors who needlessly tell patients grim or frightening facts about proposed treatment. "*That stupid doctor*", they say, "*why did he have to tell my mother — frightened enough already — about something terrible, if it is very unlikely that it will ever happen?*".

Of course, it is another story when those with the benefit of hindsight express indignation that the unfortunate victim of some remote risk was never warned about it. It would be interesting to know how consistent such critics are. When they visit friends or elderly relatives in hospital do they treat them all alike? Do they consistently discourage trust and urge them all to question staff closely in order to make sure that they are fully aware of all remote risks?

We may perhaps speak of 'anti-paternalists' as either extreme or moderate. The moderate group often imagine that they are in conflict with traditional medicine. Their criticism serves a useful purpose, but what they are really doing is little more than tilting at windmills. They ignore the fact that all good medical teachers have always spoken out against arrogance, insensitivity, discourtesy, or failure to take a proper interest in a patient's real problems and lifestyle — which is apparently what they mean by paternalism. What they should really be accusing us of is failing to live up to our ideals.

The extreme anti-paternalist, on the other hand, hates trust. Probably in his private life he is secretly very pleased when somebody trusts him. But he doesn't like to see other people being trusted. It worries him. He is even not too happy about people being given advice. He would prefer them just to be given facts and then to make up their own minds. This is in order to preserve their 'autonomy'. He forgets that if any of us in any situation (medical or non-medical) take advantage only of an expert's skill and knowledge — not his experience and judgment — we are throwing away half the value of the consultation.

What we need is better communication; more explanation for those who need it, less for those who don't; and greater empathy and understanding of the patient's real needs, fears, and aspirations. What we don't need is unhelpful rhetoric; a wholesale attack on trust; excessive emphasis on 'fully informed consent' and 'autonomy'; and a serious distortion of priorities with a consequent fall in standards of care.

For two reasons there has to be compromise. Firstly, because noble principles often give contradictory advice. Every patient has a right to full information. He also has a right to be treated with compassion, common sense, and respect for his dignity — a respect that is not usually enhanced by asking him, "*Do you want us to be frank about all the risks or not?*" Secondly, because we are all the prisoners of time, the more time we spend trying to explain things, the less there is for other aspects of patient care.

Who should make the compromise? Presumably it should be those members of society who have most experience of all the subtle and paradoxical ways in which human beings may react to illness and to fear; and who have had the greatest opportunity of learning, from first hand experience, when to speak out and when to keep silent. In other words, doctors and nurses, rather than philosophers or experts in ethics.

Provided, of course, that we are at least as concerned for the welfare of patients as are the rest of society. Which is not for us to judge. But even Bernard Shaw, in the famous preface to *The Doctor's Dilemma*, observed that "*doctors, if no better than other men, are certainly no worse*".

References

1. Phillips M, Dawson J. Doctors Dilemmas: medical ethics and contemporary science. Brighton, England: Harvester Press. 1985. Pp 230.

2. Faulder C. Whose body is it? The troubling issue of informed consent. London: Virago Press. 1985. See *Lancet* 1985. ii: 75.

3. Brewin TB. The cancer patient: communication and morale. *Br Med J* 1977; **ii**: 1623–27.

4. Joyce CRB, Caple G, Mason M, Reynolds E, Matthews JA. Quantitative study of doctor-patient communications. *Quart J Med* 1969; **38**: 183–94.

5. Cushner T. A conversation with Norman Cousins. *Lancet* 1980; **ii**: 527–28.

SIR —

While agreeing wholeheartedly with most of what Sir Theodore Fox says many will part company with him when he suggests that in hospital practice 'the final decision on what is desirable for the patient should not, in general, rest with the doctor who decides what is feasible'. Is not the specialist's knowledge of the discomforts and dangers involved just as relevant to a decision as his knowledge of what is feasible? Who can weigh risk against benefit better than the doctor who has made a special study of both? A colleague may suggest to him what he should do. A doctor who knows the patient better than he does may give invaluable information and advice. And, in practice, when the problem is difficult mutual discussion will usually quickly settle the matter. But the ultimate responsibility for seeing that a special treatment is in the patient's best interests must surely lie with the doctor who has the greatest experience of what is involved and has followed up the largest number of patients treated in this way.

If a doctor is truly 'concerned with people rather than with things' before he takes up his clinical specialty, he will continue to be so afterwards. Ignorance of scientific methods and specialist techniques cannot make him more humane. Knowledge of them will not make him less so.

(Letter to the Editor, *The Lancet* 1965 **ii** 950)

The patient's relatives —
interviewing them, learning from them, supporting them

Extract from Chapter 1 of
a book to be published by
Radcliffe Medical Press, Oxford

On hospital ward rounds the traditional question (after all other aspects of a serious newly diagnosed case have been discussed) has been *"And who will see the relatives?"* Or sometimes just, *"Who will tell the relatives?"* — as if 'telling' was all there was to it, a one way interview in which the relative is seen only as a receiver of bad news, a sort of passive receptacle, merely to be dealt with as kindly as possible.

But if we are to follow the golden rule (putting ourselves in the place of the relative, whether advising or explaining) we must do better than that. There needs to be a two way conversation of the kind that we would hope for if we were the relative or partner of a seriously ill person.

So it is never merely — who will see this man's wife and give her the bad news?

It is more —

- Who will explain the situation to her and answer her questions?
- Who will give her a chance to get to know us better? And hopefully let her see that we understand how she feels — and that what we want for the patient is the same as what she wants?
- Who will seek her help and hear her views about the patient and his illness?
- Who will enrol her as a vital member of the caring team and start to give her some practical advice and training?
- Who will see if she has any groundless fears or feelings of guilt?
- Who will give her confidence, moral support and encouragement?
- Who will make a preliminary assessment of the home situation?

Which is a lot of questions. And, of course, there is not always either the time or the need to consider all of them. But at least such a list emphasises that a patient's partner or relative should never be regarded as just a receiver of information, but as

- a receiver of information
- a provider of information
- an adviser
- a carer
- a victim

At times all these roles are equally important. At other times one is strongly predominant, but even in the briefest interview it is best to give at least a moment's thought to all of them. This is the secret of successfully 'seeing the relatives'.

In any serious situation the wise doctor, nurse, or social worker will also want to assess each relative — both as a potential carer and as a potential sufferer and victim. Has she had experience of similar situations? What seems to be her psychological state and her physical health and strength?

Ideally, the hospital doctor would always discuss such things with the family doctor. If they can do so, then both benefit, especially the specialist. But all too often neither can find the time for it.

So it's all quite complex and there seldom seems to be enough time to deal adequately with every aspect mentioned, or with every way in which we might be of help. Which contrasts with the remark of a colleague who once asked me, when he saw that I was speaking on this subject, *"How will you fill 25 minutes, talking about the patient's relatives?"*

Teaching and learning

Perhaps he meant that many insights and strategies in the field of communication come mainly from experience and are almost too subtle to teach. If so, I have a certain sympathy with this traditional view. Good communication, whether with patients or relatives, comes naturally to some people, though there is always room for improvement. For various reasons, others find it much harder. To a considerable extent, no matter how well taught, it must always be dependant on personality, on ingrained empathy and on an innate approach to illness and distress that ought to help entry to medical school.*

However, recent work by McGuire and others — mostly concerned with patients rather than relatives — suggests that, even though this is undeniably a very different matter to the teaching of, say, anatomy or pharmacology, real improvement can result from new teaching techniques. Perhaps in groups, discussing a video of how the trainee performs when interviewing either an actual patient or relative or an actor playing the part.

Advice may be given by specialists in the art of communication, psychiatrists, or psychologists. Or by those with the greatest experience of giving bad news to the relatives of, say, cancer patients. Ask the nursing staff which doctors do it best. They know. But those who teach must also be willing and able to discuss with others how they have learned from their mistakes; and this doesn't always follow.

In lectures there is an interesting problem. Most students, who will avidly write down biochemical or similar hard data given to them, will immediately stop taking notes when offered various ways of talking to anxious relatives.

Yet such advice is no more than the offering of approaches to try in different situations. Some of the things suggested will suit the personality of some doctors and nurses, but not that of others. Each medical student and young doctor needs to try them for themselves. And they must constantly seek the feedback that tells them the effect on the relative of what they said.

Learning by example

Learning by example gets less mention these days. But much can be learned just from being with someone who has plenty of experience of talking to relatives — and who does it well. Don't forget that some of those who are best at it would have great difficulty giving a lecture on the subject.

This doesn't mean that you have to copy slavishly everything you hear said or see done. However good the person setting an example, only an unthinking

---

*FOOTNOTE   So why not two or three weeks of compulsory unpaid hospital work for all aspiring medical students to observe how they get on with patients and their anxious relatives? I've never been able to understand why this is not done. It should surely count for something whenever competing applicants are of similar academic standing.

zombie would do that. Apart from the fact that nobody gets it right every time, it is not only patients and relatives who vary; doctors do, too.

Moreover a student can actually learn from watching poor communication, *badly* done. You note the ineffectiveness or the harm — and you vow that when it comes to your turn you will not so easily omit what should have been said, nor say (or at least not say so clumsily) what you feel would have been better left *unsaid*.

Finally, relatives themselves, though they may not know it, are always teaching us something. Not just some relatives, but all of them, for no relatives and no two situations are ever exactly alike. And if we approach our work in the right way we never stop learning from them.

Concise communication

All students should be taught by example and discussion that there is an art in warm, effective, concise communication.

Too much talk and writing these days contains almost as much rhetoric as practical advice — *"time must be found for as much listening and counselling as each patient and relative needs, because this is their right"* — that sort of thing is not very valuable when it comes to deciding on priorities when under pressure.

Moreover it may encourage the idea that the same amount of time must be given to every patient and relative, which is wasteful and denies attention to those who need it most.

The very word counselling seems to imply that a lot of time must be set aside; that only a few minutes in a serious situation is an insult. To go down this road is not making the best use of available time.

And even if a doctor or nurse has all the time in the world, it is doubtful if a long interview should be given to every relative, because —

- Some relatives prefer a brisk business like approach, with a minimum of chat.
- Some may resent any enquiry about their personal problems.
- There is always a risk that mentioning something that the relative was not worrying about (until now) will trigger a fresh anxiety.

Suggesting that a long session is always needed may also encourage people to opt out and refer a patient for specialised advice and counselling when a few minutes of warm positive communication could transform the situation and provide all that is needed. Or, if not all that is needed, then at least anything more should have a low priority.

As discussed later, for those who are not blind to the essential elements of feedback, it is often written all over the patient's face either that they are already well pleased and encouraged with what has been said, or that more listening and advice are required.

Getting started

- So far as possible always grasp the essential facts of each case before, not after, the relative enters. Personal data — age, job, family — not just medical data. A good memory for detail is a priceless asset for a doctor. Nothing kills empathy so much as reading case notes in the presence of the person you are interviewing. When this is unavoidable, be sure to ask permission and apologise for having to do it.

- When there is serious news to be given to relatives, it is even more important than usual to stand up immediately they enter the room and, if possible, take a step or two towards them. Don't just let them come to you. Be glad to see them. Move towards them. Perhaps thank them for coming to see you . Don't let them get the feeling that they are an unwelcome intrusion. This is not just a matter of courtesy, it shows that you accept the challenge of giving bad news and you are not afraid to face it.

- It goes without saying that, if doctor and relative have not met before, an important part of what should be normal courtesy is for the doctor to introduce herself and give the relative her name. In the hospital environment many relatives these days will also want to know the status of the person they are seeing and their position in the team and this should be made plain.

- As you take their arm or shake their hand (but be sensitive, some may prefer you not to) steer them to a seat. Address them by whatever name and style you guess they will prefer, but it's probably best when meeting for the first time — especially if the relative is elderly — to be fairly formal.

- Even when the situation to be discussed is grim, a slight but warm smile of understanding will nearly always be appreciated. Anything less is liable to make you seem cold and remote.

Then (not always, but frequently) a quick word about something quite mundane and normal — the weather, or an item in the news that everyone is talking about, or the difficulty of finding somewhere to park a car, something like that. Almost in a totally relaxed, natural way, as if there was nothing serious on the agenda. But not quite. There should be just a hint of what is to come.

How can such trivial small talk be appropriate in a serious situation? I have even seen it claimed that this is a common failing of doctors and that it is never appropriate. But anyone who says this can have little experience of the surprisingly powerful benefit that often follows if it is done in the right way. Presumably it cuts down fear and tension by its friendly normality, puts the relative more at her ease, and reduces fear. And because it shows that the doctor is human.

But, like everything else suggested in this book, if done the wrong way it can be useless or even harmful. One mistake, for example, would be to take too long over it. This could suggest either an insensitive failure to appreciate that the relative's mind is in turmoil, wondering what is going to be said — or it could mean an overall awkwardness and embarrassment. Worse still, a wish to postpone for as long as possible the serious things that sooner or later have to be said . .

Hopes and fears of the elderly cancer patient

Reprinted from
Cancer in the Elderly, 1990, Chapter 3,
Eds: Caird & Brewin, pubs: Wright, London

Hopes and fears are inevitably intertwined. Though some hopes may be very positive, a hope that something will not happen is not fundamentally different to a fear that it will. However, even a negative hope implies a calmer emotion than fear. Intense fear is a form of suffering; to relieve it is as rewarding as to relieve pain. Whatever the age of the patient and whatever the diagnosis, all doctors and nurses spend much of their time reassuring patients in one way or another. Nowhere is this more important than in the case of the elderly patient with cancer. No matter how bad the outlook, there are always truthful ways of improving morale and reducing fear.

Apart from fear, the most obvious psychological symptoms to afflict the elderly cancer patient are depression and sadness (occasionally accompanied by bitterness and self-pity). Though depression and sadness overlap, they are not the same thing. True depression may respond to antidepressant drugs. In other cases, side-effects (such as making an already dry mouth even dryer) — and doubtful benefit — argue against their use in all but a few patients. But as with so many other remedies, valid comparisons (randomized to prevent false conclusions due to selection bias) are badly needed to help settle the question of when these drugs help and when they do more harm than good.

Sadness is something we cannot do a lot about. Human life must always include partings and other losses of various kinds, sometimes very hard to bear. In recent years there has perhaps been a danger of some especially dedicated nurses and other health workers spending too much precious time trying to relieve all forms of unhappiness; and then feeling guilty if they fail, thus needlessly adding to the stress of their work. This is the opposite error to not realizing how much can be done. Fortunately, not every patient needs — or, indeed, will welcome — the prolonged listening and counselling that is so helpful to others. Many can be greatly helped in a fairly short time; and perhaps this point is not sufficiently recognized in our current teaching.

Alongside hopes, fears, sadness and depression, may go regrets; and these are often tinged (or maybe heavily overlaid) with guilt. Even when there is a very real chance of cure, the patient who is told that a form of cancer has been found may at first feel convinced that his life is finished. Suddenly he sees the way ahead leading straight to a door marked 'Exit'. If he is elderly, this ought not to come as such a great shock, but it often does. He may then suffer pangs of regret about missed opportunities, about achieving less in life than he had hoped, about failing to realize how quickly time was passing, about not being fully reconciled after some family quarrel, and so on.

This chapter will concentrate mainly on fear, because this is such a common and distressing symptom; and because it can be helped to a surprising degree, both in the short term and the long term, without drugs and without any pretence or deception. '*I don't know what you said to her, but she has been a different person since you spoke to her*', suggests that the right kind of understanding and empathy was shown and that the right things were said — at the right time and in the right way.

Realistic communication

To be both effective against fear and also economical in time, all communication needs to be realistic. Joyce *et al* (1969) and Ley (1977) have shown the following:

1. Immediately after an interview with a doctor, patients are often unable to repeat many of the things that have just been said to them.

2. The first thing said has the best chance of being remembered (a very important practical point).

3. Less is remembered when the prognosis is bad (presumably due either to shock or to denial).

4. The more that is said the less is recalled, not only proportionally but also absolutely.

If this is true of unselected patients, it is likely to be doubly true of the elderly; especially the very elderly, perhaps not hearing as well as they would like, perhaps finding it difficult to concentrate on what is being said to them (or to recall the question that was in their mind just a moment ago), and often confused by new surroundings. Such a patient, whose current mental capacity may be such that she cannot be expected to understand and remember more than a very few sentences may still be capable of apparently normal and polite responses — for example when asked how she is feeling. It is then all too easy for a busy doctor not to realize the true state of affairs; and to waste time and perhaps confuse the patient with inappropriate communication.

We also need to be realistic about the possibly devastating emotional effect of certain words (something that will vary a lot according to the person we are speaking to, making a sensitive assessment during each interview vital) and about the very real danger of being misunderstood. A sensitive doctor tries to allow for a patient not listening properly to everything he says; and, if it turns out later that the patient got the wrong impression, will not immediately blame him for distorting or misquoting, but will learn from such experiences just how difficult the art of communication can be.

Even when there is good recall and no misquoting, it is quite common for a patient or relative, when talking later to a friend, to comment. *'He didn't actually say so, but my impression is that what he really thinks is...'* and then go on to say something that may, for example, be far more pessimistic or far more optimistic than the doctor intended. The impression given is therefore as important as the words used; and here such things as emphasis, tone of voice, and facial expression play a vital role.

Fear in various situations

There are many different situations to be considered. Even before the diagnosis has been made, when tests are being done and cancer is only a possibility, there may be intense fear. But naturally, for many, the worst moment is the moment of being told the diagnosis; worse than anything that comes before or after (though, interestingly, those who have suffered from recurrent cancerphobia for much of their life are among those who may now become surprisingly calm and stoical).

How the patient is told is important. Quite apart from the obvious point that the doctor himself must not look or sound frightened, quite small variations in the words used may make a big difference to how much fear they cause. For example, *'The tests show a kind of cancer, but at least it's not as serious as some kinds, and we know now what to do*', said firmly and sincerely, may be much less frightening than, '*I'm afraid you have cancer*'. Moreover, this first way of giving the bad news, so far from putting a misleading gloss on the situation, probably gives a more truthful impression than the second.

During remission (when nobody knows if the patient is cured or not) fear is a common cause of a needlessly low quality of life. Logically, many elderly cancer patients in remission ought to be no more afraid of the future than are elderly patients with heart disease. Either could relapse and die at any time. Moreover those in remission after treatment for cancer have an advantage: they can at least hope that they are cured.

And many of them are. Not always with all their disease eradicated, it is true. But provided that there are no further symptoms due to the cancer, and death, when it occurs, is due to another cause, such patients have had maximum benefit from the treatment and so should be regarded as cured. Small untreated cancer deposits in the body are compatible with perfect health, perhaps for years (for example, in the case of elderly men with carcinoma of the prostate, or elderly women with occult metastases from carcinoma of the breast). But, sadly, so deeply ingrained in human nature is a strange, special fear of cancer, and so unpleasant to the average patient is the thought of any cancer cells surviving, that peace of mind is easier to achieve when a patient is in remission after treatment for heart disease than it is after treatment for cancer.

The two main ways of coping with this problem of anxiety in patients in remission are in sharp contrast with each other (Brewin 1986). One is to remain a cancer patient, so to speak: to read books and leaflets about cancer, perhaps join a self help group, and strive for a feeling of being 'in control' by adopting various diets or other stratagems (either 'orthodox' or 'alternative'), whether or not there is any convincing evidence to support them. The other approach, which many elderly cancer patients will probably prefer, is to become as quickly as possible an ex-cancer patient:

1. Not 'fighting' the cancer, but so far as possible forgetting it.
2. Relying more on a philosophical acceptance of whatever fate has in store.
3. Knowing that death will come sooner or later, either from the cancer or from some other cause, but not wanting to think about it or talk about it.
4. Taking each day as it comes, grateful for what has been achieved, even if nothing can be promised.

Other situations include the fear caused by recurrence or metastasis (perhaps after many months, or even years, of hoping that the condition has been cured) — often a devastating blow to morale, but by no means always the end of all hope — and the fear that may arise in terminal illness, as discussed in Chapter 7.

Different fears

Fear is a surprisingly unpredictable emotion. Not just in the medical world, but in many situations in life in general, it is common to feel, 'How strange that I don't feel any fear'; or, on another occasion, 'How absurd that I should feel so afraid'. Fear is not always logical or related to prognosis. Patients may be less frightened when they learn that their cancer has become incurable than they were when there was a good chance of cure.

Another common mistake is not to realize that the hopes and fears of many ill patients, especially many elderly cancer patients, may be focused more on the short term than the long term. The young doctor, like many healthy members of the public, may feel that the immediate future is of little importance compared with the long-term future. He or she may underestimate the enormous value to the ill or frightened patient of reassurance and encouragement about what to expect in the coming days and weeks (forgetting for the moment next year or the year after that). Just the hope of soon feeling better is what occupies the mind of many patients.

How do we decide what the patient is mainly afraid of? Sometimes it is a good idea to ask directly. But often it is kinder and better not to be too blunt. Relatives may be able to help. But even the patient is not always sure. We must not make the mistake of thinking that every ill person can analyse their feelings in a logical way. Nor should we underestimate the value of non-specific ways of relieving non-specific fears.

However, there are good reasons to pick up clues whenever possible. Firstly, because one of the fears mentioned sometimes strongly predominates over others. Secondly, because reassurance in areas where it is not needed may actually create, rather than diminish, anxiety. It is often helpful for members of the caring team to record for the benefit of others a remark made by a patient about a particular hope or fear. If this is done very briefly, in quotation marks and without comment, it is both quicker and more valuable than attempting to record 'What the patient has been told'.

When a particular fear has been identified (for example, fear of death within the next few months), indirect reassurance may be more effective than direct. For example, *'Where do you think you will go for a holiday or a weekend break next summer?'* is a friendly, valid and perfectly honest question, whenever there is a reasonable chance that such a thing will be possible, even though nothing can be promised. Equally valuable is to give some indication of the frequency of check ups in the coming months or years, if all goes well. Such an approach can quickly restore at least a measure of hope to a patient who has been lying awake the night before, convinced that she is finished, with no chance of ever again enjoying life with her family.

Some common fears

Common fears of the elderly cancer patient can be summarized under five headings:

1. Fear of death and dying.
2. Fear of cancer.
3. Fear of hospitals, tests and treatment.
4. Fear of becoming helpless and a burden to others.
5. Fear of being deserted.

These key fears will now be discussed, together with some of the ways that experience shows can be particularly valuable in lessening them, or even abolishing them.

Fear of death and dying

These two fears should be kept separate. Many patients fear one more than the other. So far as fear of death is concerned, some may dread it *"as children fear to go in the dark"* (Bacon, 1597). Probably it has always been like this. *"Old men complain of age and pray for death"*, says one of the characters in a play by Euripides, *"but let death come close and not one of them still wants to die"* (quoted by Garland 1987). 'Not one' is certainly an exaggeration, but we must be careful not to assume that a patient, however old or ill, is tired of life. It may be so, it may not. Some, as mentioned in Chapter 5, have a special reason for wanting to live a little longer. Even those with apparently nothing to look forward to may badly want to hang onto life, perhaps from fear of the unknown.

As to fear of the act of dying, some of the public seem to imagine that death is as likely as birth to be associated with distress, which is certainly not so. Most elderly cancer patients are peaceful at the end, if not throughout their illness. Occasionally, specific reassurance on this point is called for, as described in Chapter 7.

Fear of cancer

Needless fears are very common. They include fear that the cancer is hereditary and may be passed on to another member of the family; that it is infectious; that it is rarely, if ever, completely cured; that it is always painful, always unnatural and horrible; or even that it is a kind of punishment or stigma.

As with all forms of reassurance, positive statements are better than negative ones: '*This sort of thing is quite common at your age, it could happen to anyone. Lead as normal a life as possible; see your friends; have your grandchildren visit you as usual. And let's hope you will respond as well to treatment as did another patient of mine in your position*'. This kind of thing is preferable to, '*Try not to worry, it's not hopeless, it's not infectious, and you mustn't think it's necessarily going to be painful*'. Note that these two approaches are equally truthful and equally sincere, but that the first is far more likely to reduce fear and improve morale than the second.

Fear of hospitals, tests and treatment

This fear is commonly underestimated. Many elderly patients delay seeking advice, not because they don't realize that their symptoms could be due to a cancer requiring urgent attention, but because they fear the treatment. With some kinds of cancer, delay may make little difference to the chance of cure, but may nevertheless be the cause of months of unnecessary anxiety and of a needlessly poor quality of life that could have been avoided. With others delay may mean that cure is no longer possible.

It is not just the patient's fear that she may never see home again after admission to hospital; that she will never wake up again after an anaesthetic; that radiotherapy will be frightening; or that chemotherapy will cause vomiting and loss of hair. She may know from previous experience that even just lying on a rock hard X-ray table while waiting for a doctor to check the films can be a great ordeal. She may dread repeated blood tests, or the embarrassment and indignity of some hospital procedures.

Fear of a different kind may arise at the thought of admission to a Hospice, a Marie Curie Home, or some similar institution. Elderly people, who many times over the years have seen such a unit mentioned in obituary columns (and who have perhaps given money in response to appeals, but have never seen inside) may greatly fear going in.

This is in marked contrast to how they are likely to react if they can be persuaded to go. Then, the warm welcome they receive, the surprisingly cheerful, 'normal' atmosphere that is often achieved, and the immediate wholehearted concentration on their symptoms, rather than on seemingly endless investigations, will very often (in spite of seeing other patients die) improve their morale, rather than depress it; and they will often be a lot happier than they were in hospital. They may even prefer being here to being in their own home. Perhaps mainly because of feeling safer, knowing that trained staff are constantly at hand. But perhaps also because there are always people to talk to. The popular idea of everyone preferring to die in their own home forgets that some homes are lonely places; that many partners or other companions are themselves elderly and under great strain, which adds to the patient's distress; and that not all homes have a happy atmosphere, even though many do.

Fear of becoming helpless and a burden to others

Many elderly people hate the feeling of being 'on the scrap heap', and of no use to anyone. The elderly patient with cancer is in even greater danger of feeling that he is now just a burden to others; and perhaps not only a burden, but a depressing, offensive burden, for example if he has a colostomy or an ulcerated tumour.

This fear can be countered in three main ways. Firstly, a very brief note, for other staff to see, mentioning anything of interest in the elderly patient's present or past life, even if totally irrelevant from a strictly medical point of view. This gives him or her some dignity and status, perhaps as an expert of some kind in former days, perhaps with an interesting story to tell. The older that patients are, the more important it is that everyone caring for them should know what their occupation was (never just that they are retired), or perhaps how large a family they reared, and so on.

Secondly, by asking patients for their opinion about something — better still, for their advice on some subject in which they have more experience than we do — we help to restore both their confidence in themselves, and their trust in us. They need to know that we see them, not just as cases of cancer in old age, their lives finished, but as living individuals and personalities, often still able to help others, even though it may be only in very small ways.

Thirdly, we must show a sincere interest in all symptoms, but particularly those connected with bowels or bladder or anything that the patient fears may be repugnant to us. And we must be glad to see such a patient; happy to be near him, to touch him firmly and examine him closely; at the same time letting him know that his symptoms, and how they respond to various remedies, will help us to deal with other patients with similar problems.

Fear of being deserted
It is a sad fact that some doctors, some relatives and friends, and even some nurses, are embarrassed and awkward in the presence of cancer patients (particularly if the outlook is bad) and do their best to avoid them. All very elderly people have the same effect on some people, so it is hardly surprising if the problem is even greater if they have cancer. Probably we have all been guilty of this sometimes, to some extent. Presumably one reason is that we are forcibly reminded of our own mortality. At any rate, this is one of the fears of the patient; that he will be deserted; that his friends and his carers will want to avoid him; or that they will visit him at first, but soon stop coming.

Two of the best ways to combat this problem have already been suggested — interest in the patient as a person (his cancer and his age don't make him any less interesting as a human being) and interest in his symptoms and what can be done about them. A third and vital point is that whenever a doctor proposes to see a patient less frequently in future, this should always be put to him in a suitably positive way — in other words as good news. It must never be done without explanation and never in a cold or awkward way that might be interpreted as loss of interest.

The old chestnut: should a doctor tell?

In recent years (in some countries, notably the USA) there has been quite a big swing against the traditional policy of not usually using the word cancer when telling patients their diagnosis. This change is one that many patients welcome, and which probably improves public attitudes ('knowledge is the antidote to fear'); but which for others has serious disadvantages, such as excessive shock and mental anguish, various misconceptions, and extreme pessimism, even when the doctor makes great efforts to counteract this.

Frankness about the diagnosis of cancer and frankness about the prognosis are often discussed together, as if they were inseparable, but they are not.

Current practice with regard to when to spell out a bad prognosis to a patient (whether or not he or she really seems to want this) has changed much less in recent years than has open use of the word cancer. Many elderly cancer patients, especially those with little hope of cure, seem to have an instinctive feeling that it might be wiser not to ask about their prognosis; and many experienced doctors and nurses (including many working in Hospices or Marie Curie Homes) feel that, when this is the case, it is usually best to respect it. Other patients prefer to bring it all out into the open; and a doctor should be equally comfortable with either attitude, always bearing in mind that patients quite often change from wanting to discuss these things to not wanting to (perhaps then talking exactly as if no frank discussion had ever taken place), so that a sensitive, flexible respect for the patient's current attitude is vital. *'What the patient has been told'* is of much less importance.

Some of those who don't ask about their prognosis are no doubt unconsciously using the protective 'denial' mechanism; some probably prefer not to risk an answer to their question that might take away all hope; while some have a very good idea of just how serious the situation is, but prefer not to discuss it. Certainly, many cancer patients — especially, perhaps, elderly ones — may have a very warm and good relationship with those looking after them without diagnosis or prognosis ever being discussed. This is something that those with little or no experience of looking after such patients find very surprising and difficult to understand. There is, in fact, a considerable gulf between public assumptions and reality. There is also probably a sizeable gap between what critics say in public debate on this subject, and how they feel when an elderly friend or relative of their own develops cancer.

Non-specific ways of counteracting fear

Although the identification of a specific fear may be very valuable, there are many ways in which good communication can reduce fear in a broad, non-specific way. The following are examples.

Empathy, explanation and efficiency
Patients warm to a doctor who seems to have at least some idea of how they feel and of their hopes, fears and priorities. This is one of the most essential ingredients of a good relationship. It should lead, almost automatically, not only to a desire to help, but to help in a way that is appropriate for this particular patient.

Whatever is said or not said about diagnosis and prognosis, much of the fear caused by symptoms disappears when they are explained. It makes sense to an anxious patient (and may rid him of needless fears) to hear that his shortness of breath is due to one of his lungs not functioning properly; or that his nausea is due to failure of his liver to excrete waste products.

If the doctor also gives the impression of knowing exactly what needs to be done — and if, when a team of health workers is involved, there is a general feeling of efficiency — the patient will feel less anxious, safer and more confident.

Optimism and encouragement
Of great benefit to elderly cancer patients is the right kind of encouragement; a positive attitude to every problem, large or small; at least a measure of rehabilitation whenever appropriate; and a return to as normal life as possible. This is especially welcome to the patient whose cancer is inoperable or advanced and who comes from a gloomy consultant or family doctor — one who is so depressed by the diagnosis or prognosis that he shows little interest in the patient's morale or symptoms and does not seem to realize how much can be done.

There is a fundamental difference between sincere optimism and insincere optimism. Even when the outlook is very bad, optimism can still be compatible with honesty, for it may simply concentrate on certain distressing symptoms and the very real hope of relieving them.

Some patients, at times of stress, need very positive, undiluted optimism, which would be too much for another patient. A few patients thrive on a certain amount of pessimism. Every patient is different. Every situation is different. Every doctor is different. But what if everything goes badly? Will the patient and her family not feel let down, and will they not resent the previous optimism? Not usually, in my experience, provided that the optimism was of the sincere, concerned, caring variety. In fact, if there has been a good relationship, all concerned, including the doctor, share the same sadness and disappointment that things did not turn out as had been hoped.

Too much optimism is as bad as too little. It must not be overdone. But the idea that it is somehow unprofessional to be positive and optimistic, especially where cancer is concerned, must be firmly rejected. If done sincerely, with emphasis on the fact that nothing can be promised (I never knew a patient to be depressed by this warning; it is hope that is longed for, not promises) optimism and a positive attitude can boost morale and can improve the chances of symptom relief, with or without rehabilitation. Patient, staff and family must all be told the aim of treatment, how it helped another patient (mention of one is often enough) and how other treatments are available, should this one fail.

Small talk and humour
Small talk or humour might seem at first to be irrelevant, inappropriate, or in bad taste in a serious situation. And to be very unlikely to help. But in reality such things may make quite a big difference. A few words about something completely non-medical have been shown to make an important contribution to medical consultations (Korsch, Freemon and Nagrete 1971). Sometimes, when this is done, doctor and patient will discover that they have something in common, such as having been on holiday in the same part of the world. Perhaps both have a grandchild, or like to watch the same sport. And there is no doubt that humour (even very 'black' humour) can sometimes dissolve fear in a most remarkable way. But only experience and a feel for these things can tell the doctor when humour is appropriate; when it would be distasteful; and when it would be a disaster.

Elderly patients particularly appreciate a doctor who takes an interest, however brief, in the achievements of their children or grandchildren. If in a patient's house, always have a look at any wedding groups or old prints. Ask what the price of milk or bread or a short bus ride was in those days. It doesn't take a minute. And never forget that every old person was once young, perhaps a keen cyclist, or an enthusiastic ballroom dancer; and that many still feel young (on some days, anyway).

All this must be sincere; a natural part of the doctor's personality; and, in a sense, spontaneous. It must never be artificial or forced. If it is, it won't work. And it must never be a substitute for serious conversation, if that is what is needed.

Why should this sort of thing so often help? Why is it an almost essential ingredient, however brief, of even the most serious consultations and interviews, if honest hope is to be given and fears eased? Presumably because talking about the sort of things that normal healthy people talk about helps the patient to think of herself as still in the normal world and not in the nightmare world of 'the cancer victim'. Because it is a form of diversion (any kind of diversion can help fear, just as it can help pain). Because it emphasizes that the doctor is human. And because this is the conversation of life, not death. Whatever the reason there is no doubt of the value of a brief, friendly chat about nothing in particular, usually at the end of the consultation, sometimes at the start.

Unspoken communication
A sincere smile, a firm handclasp, an unhurried manner, and many intangible messages conveyed by the way the doctor walks towards the patient or sits down beside her, are especially important in the case of the cancer patient who is elderly. Such things can carry a powerful impression both of friendly warmth and understanding, and also of the sort of confidence and efficiency that convinces the patient (whether or not she remembers exactly what was said) that she is in safe hands.

Touch (which is likely to be especially valuable if there is any degree of blindness or deafness) can be a most effective antidote to fear. But remember that even the doctor with the warmest hands and the kindest heart has to be careful not to overdo the handholding. Not all elderly patients appreciate it. Not with every doctor, anyway. Fortunately, as in happier and less professional situations in life, provided that reasonable sensitivity is shown and nothing taken for granted, we usually quickly know where we stand and whether or not we have done the right thing. Though lacking the precision of, say, Boyle's law, it seems safe to assume that, when a doctor (of either sex) takes a patient's hand, the strength and the duration of the counterpressure, if any, exerted by the patient, are roughly proportional to how badly such contact was needed and how much it is appreciated.

References

Bacon, F. (1597) *Essays*, Dent (1972 edn), London, p.6

Brewin, T.B. (1986) In *Coping with Cancer Stress* (ed. B.A. Stoll), Martinus Nijhoff, Dordrecht (Netherlands), p. 83

Garland, R. (1987) *History Today*, **37**, 12

Joyce, C.R.B., Caple, G., Mason, M. et al. (1969) *Q. J. Med.*, **38**, 183

Korsch, B.M. Freemon, B. and Negrete, V.F. (1971) *Am. J. Dis. Child.*, **121**, 110

Ley, P. (1977) In *Introducing Psychology* (ed. J.C. Coleman), Routledge and Kegan Paul, London, p. 321

Not TLC
but FPI

Reprinted from
the Journal of the Royal Society of Medicine,
1990, Vol 83, pages 172–175

There is nothing wrong with tender loving care, of course, so far as it goes. Whether the outlook is good or bad, many of us who have been on the receiving end know how cool and comforting it can be. And if the prognosis is 'hopeless' — for example in many cases of advanced cancer — TLC is doubly important. No doubt about that. But it misses out too much; and it may suggest to the hospital consultant, or even the family doctor, that this is not what all his years of training were for; that he is now scarcely needed.

Friendly professional interest (FPI) gives a better idea of what is wanted in advanced or terminal illness. Basic, good quality, FPI need not take up a lot of a doctor's time; and is often enough by itself to help every kind of symptom, physical or psychological. Sometimes much more is needed: perhaps a lot more listening; perhaps calling in others with special skills or experience. But for the doctor with many other demands on his time, just FPI is the vital thing. Much needless suffering and low morale results when it is missing.

In one study[1], when large numbers of bereaved relatives were interviewed, a widow spoke of how *'the doctor came and said, "there's no point in visiting your husband, there's nothing we can do for him".'* Then she changed to another doctor, *'and he was marvellous... he put my husband's mind at rest ... if you've got some moral support you can carry on. He visited him once a week'.*

She is not just being polite, is she? She is not saying, *'there was really nothing he could do, but at least he called in occasionally'.* No: he only visited once a week, yet this transformed the situation, not only for the patient, but for the relative, too. No mention here of multidisciplinary care; no calling in of individuals or teams specially trained in terminal care or counselling the dying; no daily visits. For this man's wife the situation may have been heartbreaking, but regular weekly support and encouragement from her new doctor was all she needed to enable her to cope. Some people ask for so little. The tragedy is when they don't get it. The first doctor didn't understand this and did nothing. But the second one did. And look what a difference it made.

How did he do it? We don't know. We can only guess. But I suggest that it may well have been just basic FPI; that when he made his weekly visit, he may not have been in the house for more than 15 minutes. She did the TLC. He provided the FPI. That was the team. And the modest total time it took shows how cost effective FPI can be.

Though in some ways the situation is different, the same thing applies in hospital wards. Any competent consultant should be aware of the importance of remaining friendly and professional, no matter how good the nurses and junior medical staff. On his formal rounds — perhaps after discussing an undiagnosed patient in the next bed — he comes to a patient who may soon die of advanced cancer. Quite naturally and openly the differential diagnosis and treatment of **each symptom** is then thoroughly discussed. There is no need to start talking in a low voice, as if in church, just because the prognosis is so bad. It should be no harder to avoid saying something that would be needlessly hurtful to the patient (or to other patients who might overhear) than it was at the previous bed, where incurable cancer may well have been one of a number of possibilities.

And then, if he can possibly manage it, even just once a week, for a few minutes (by himself, or with one other doctor or nurse, not more, and preferably after discarding his white coat) the consultant has a few words with the patient; and is glad to do so. This less formal visit is powerful medicine for low morale. And if the relatives are there when he comes, so much the better. Quite apart from any exchange of views it is good that they should see his (or her) easy, friendly, yet interested and professional, approach.

It all sounds fairly simple and obvious; yet I have never met a single nurse with an interest in this field, who wasn't privately surprised and disappointed by the poor showing of so many otherwise proficient doctors encountered in the course of her career. Very often the problem seems to be not so much a lack of concern or awareness as a sort of mental block, affecting to some extent at least 50% of the medical profession, a block that neutralizes friendliness, paralyses normal professional competence, and switches off interest. Why is this? Is this type of work not just part of our job?

Friendly

The ability of one person to lend strength to another (not just in medicine, but also in the way that a good leader does, for example when men or women face possible death in some other kind of threat or disaster) is a mystery that nobody entirely understands. But, for my money, in medical situations — especially advanced cancer — just being natural and friendly has a lot to do with it. Look at the way some hospital cleaners and porters boost the morale of frightened patients. Do they have special under-standing, spiritual inspiration, or powers of leadership? Not usually. How many communication and counselling courses have they attended? None. They are just natural and relaxed, with friendly good humour and no awkwardness or embarrassment.

With advanced cancer a climate of 'normality' (for at least part of the time, especially at the end of a visit or consultation) is nearly always helpful. Perhaps a mention of holidays, children, or grandchildren; a quick word about the weather, or last night's football results. Perhaps a brief exchange of views or experiences. Maybe some problem that doctor and patient share. But be careful — 'the trouble with seeing my doctor', one patient told me, 'is that we talk mainly about his troubles, we never seem to get around to mine'.

Professional friendship is not quite the same as ordinary friendship, but much that applies still holds true. A friend is warm and welcoming at each meeting. A friend pays small compliments. A friend has at least some idea of how the patient feels; some idea of what she has been going through; understands how her moods vary (maybe hope one day, despair the next). A friend listens; knows the value of a little praise; asks how she can help. A friend is just as ready to talk seriously (if that is what the patient wants) as to joke or gossip. A really supportive friend doesn't go over the top emotionally, but is always concerned; doesn't stay too long; knows when to be silent; doesn't ask too many questions. A doctor should follow suit.

Professional

"*May I suggest*", said a letter in *New Society* a few years ago, "*that Medicine concentrates on its task of finding cures… and leaves others — better qualified — to ensure a good death*". Whoever wrote this either knew little about the subject, or had been very unlucky. Professional efficiency helps the patient to feel safe. And when he feels safe he begins to relax. And when he relaxes many of his physical as well as his psychological symptoms improve, he sleeps better, and he is able to turn to the diversions that can do so much for his morale. The amateur, no matter how kind, will be all at sea in several important respects.

How the patient is approached ought to depend on how he is feeling that day, not on his prognosis. At least some of the questions asked should be open ended[2], showing both concern and interest, and including, not so much questions, as invitations — *"tell me more about these nightmares you've been having. I'm interested in that ..."*. Tactful interruption and re-routeing of the conversation can still be practised, whenever time is at a premium. Being a good listener is as much a matter of quality as quantity.

A common error is to cease routine clinical examinations. They are now thought to be inappropriate. But it depends how they are done. Most patients feel safer and happier if they have an occasional brisk and business-like, yet gentle and respectful, examination of the whole body. It stresses to them that they have not been abandoned, that the doctor is still anxious not to miss anything that could be corrected or prevented. And this is also a chance to lay firm, calm, caring, unhurried hands on all parts of the body, blending professional efficiency with the age-old power of touch to give comfort; at the same time sending a clear signal to the patient that we don't think of him as in any way repugnant, unclean or infectious.

Another mistake is to be so upset by the prognosis that symptom assessment seems almost an irrelevance This is wrong. If a patient has a new pain (or any other symptom) the same sort of questions need to be asked as might be asked of a healthy patient with possible appendicitis or angina. A feeling of failure must not be allowed to paralyse the problem solving approach that exists when the patient is curable. By no means all symptoms will be due to the cancer. Quite apart from how this effects their management, appropriately worded reassurance on this score may be greatly appreciated by the patient.

Basic terminal care is something that any clinician should be able to do after going through medical school. For some years the *British National Formulary*, easily accessible to every doctor, has briefly covered some commonly neglected points. Further advice is readily available in standard textbooks; for example, the chapter in the *Oxford Textbook of Medicine* by Dame Cicely Saunders[3], who has done so much to open our eyes to what can be achieved. And when it comes to managing cancer pain with analgesics, *'the basic principles are remarkably easy to learn'*[4]. Yet a recent survey of practice in the wards of a London teaching hospital found that much of the new knowledge accumulated in the last 15 or 20 years (regarding, for example, the optimum dose and timing of morphine) had still *'not filtered across into the hospital'*[5].

Stories of needless pain are common. A young hospital doctor visited a hospice. Her patient had been suffering severe pain while in hospital and she wanted to see how she was progressing. She found her now on an adequate dose of morphine, alert and pain free. *"You could have done that — why didn't you?"* asked the Matron of the hospice, more puzzled than critical. A good question. And note that the answer was not lack of compassion. The visit showed that.

Pain is the obvious problem, but assessment doesn't stop there. As an antidote to that sinking feeling, when faced with a grim situation, try systematically going through a simple aide-memoire of points to consider and assess. 'Mind, Mouth, Mobility, Bowels, Bladder, Bedsores' is one such. This sort of check list helps to prevent human tragedy from turning a trained professional into a bumbling amateur.

To be professional we also need to be practical (something that those of us with mainly hospital experience have to be especially careful about) and, above all, positive. *'The first thing they told me'*, said a patient in a television programme, talking about her admission to a Marie Curie Home, *'was that they don't allow pain here'*. To some that will seem not quite honest and smacking too much of the language of miracles, magic and alternative medicine. But, like so much else, it depends how it is said. Its great virtue is that it shows, not just positive thinking, but professional pride and team spirit — something that is just as appropriate for a team working on symptom control, as it is for one aiming to cure. And if a doctor prefers to be more cautious, he can at least say, *'I'm not promising. Nothing works every time. But this is what has helped other patients. And if this doesn't work there are plenty of other things we can try.'*

Other aspects of being professional include:
1) understanding and being comfortable with all the subtleties of ambivalence and denial and how they may vary from day to day[3,6], so that to think of patients as consistently 'knowing' or 'not knowing' their outlook is not very realistic or helpful;
2) appropriate explanation to patients of the anatomy and physiology of their symptoms;
3) getting rid of needless fears; and
4) having a proper sense of priorities (for example, it should be obvious

that, if a cancer is advanced and incurable, then an ingrowing toe nail, or a toothache, or constipation, or wax in the ears, may be far more important than anything the cancer is doing).

Interest

Neither the patient or his symptoms become any less interesting just because the prognosis is bad. Patients like to be looked after by a doctor who is obviously both interested and pleased when a symptom improves. Many patients also like to feel that when they give their opinion on the value of a remedy they are helping to contribute knowledge that will help other patients. So tell them this.

And we need to be interested not just in symptoms, but in the patient as a person. As soon as more pressing and professional matters have been dealt with, a little reminiscing about the past, no matter how brief, helps morale. Its very irrelevance seems to give it strength. Indeed, quite a high priority should be given to brief documentation of something that is medically irrelevant, but important to the patient. Just three or four words in the case record may be enough. Then others — after glancing at the patient's notes — are not only familiar with the salient medical facts, but can also say to the patient when they see her, *'I hear you were once on television'*, or *'I see you have a daughter nursing in Canada — which part?'* Something very brief of that kind.

Interest in patients as people also often leads to increased respect for them. Ask them for their advice about something. And remember that they may still appreciate being consulted about problems other than their own. For example, it may be appropriate to say to a very ill patient, *'We'd like your help. Do you think your wife is getting enough sleep? What do you think we should do about it? You know her better than we do'*.

Some general points

FPI suits any age, any race, any culture, any faith (or none), any 'philosophy of care' — and any prognosis. It is also exactly the same for patients who "know" as for those who don't. Why shouldn't it be? Why should either the prognosis, or the knowledge that the patient has of it, have the slightest effect on the need to be natural, the need to be professional, the need to be interested in the patient and in his current symptoms? If the patient seems to want to discuss just exactly how bad the prognosis is, something must be done about it. But that is another story[3,6]. The point to stress here is that, no matter how this particular dilemma is tackled, discussion of it must always be *in addition* to FPI, never in place of it.

FPI must be sustained. Many patients live 'longer than expected' — which often just means longer than average (for their situation and their type of cancer). If the interval between visits is to be increased, this must be explained in a positive way, for example on the basis of improved symptom control. It must never look like loss of interest; and the patient must know where he stands and when to expect the next visit. A phone call can be a great ally, sometimes taking the place of a visit. And remember, when phoning, that to speak only to the patient's partner or relative is as bad as the '*does he take sugar?*' attitude that insults the blind or the severely disabled. We forget how many patients now have a phone at their bedside; or a cordless phone that can be brought to their chair. Talk to them. Even a very brief phone call can contain the three essential ingredients of FPI. Provided it does — and provided the patient does not have some particular reason for needing a visit rather than a chat — it can be a most effective and powerful form of moral support.

Conscientious doctors who make dutiful visits — sometimes quite frequent ones — may fail to provide any of the three elements of FPI. '*One of the doctors in the practice calls in nearly every day*', one dying man told me, '*but it seems to be just to check that I'm still alive, they don't actually do anything, I've told them to stop coming so often*'. If these doctors had called in less often, but with real FPI, it would have given a lot more help and taken up less time. In another case a patient with advanced cancer, whose tragic terminal illness dragged on for months, asked me if I would write her doctor more cheerful letters. So I did. '*Bearing in mind all her problems there are several things I am very pleased about; true, she is weaker, but she is at least not quite as uncomfortable as she was a month ago; and her courage is an inspiration to us all*'. Something of that sort. This seemed to help. The dying patient thanked me and reported that her doctor now seemed a little happier, a little less sad. The same thing can happen in hospital. '*They meant to be kind*', said one woman after her husband had died in hospital, '*but they didn't know how to do it, they all seemed frightened*'.

The specialist in terminal care or in pain control, who privately concludes, after he has been called in, that the main problem is just a lack of simple FPI, is naturally reluctant to say so. It is more tactful for him to offer to take the patient over, and to suggest that more time, or more expertise, are needed than the non specialist can be reasonably expected to provide. This is understandable, but often misleading and may encourage neglect of basic FPI — for which there is always time, and for which no patient should ever have to wait. Equally, when a specialist of one kind or another is successful, this may be at least partly due to the fact that, for the first time, someone has shown a real interest and been friendly and positive. This makes what else the specialist has to offer — orthodox or alternative, surgical or spiritual — more difficult to assess.

So we have to watch the danger that the new specialty of Palliative Medicine (and the rapid increase in hospices and home care teams) will lead, not just to the better terminal care that everyone wants, but also to more almost automatic 'opting out' by some hospital and family doctors — and to the idea that a high percentage of patients (instead of an important minority) need hospices or other special care.

Reasons for lack of FPI and what can be done about it

Does the fault lie in the Medical Schools? If so, in the curriculum or in the teachers? Merely to be friendly and to be interested should not require any special training or 'communication skills'. Should trainees spend more time watching and learning from those doctors in every specialty who do it well? The nursing staff know who they are. Or is that too simple? Or too invidious?

Is it true, as some believe, that when the outlook is grave it takes a particular kind of person merely to be relaxed and natural and treat each symptom as a challenge? If so, can we identify them, lower a little the academic threshold for entry to medical school, and then give them some priority? Perhaps it's all in the DNA of each one of us, and one day there will be a blood test for it. Meanwhile, could we not insist on two or three weeks work in hospital for all would-be doctors — and then assess them? Those who are at ease with very ill people, and who seem to help them, could at least be preferred to others — of equal academic status — who aren't and who don't.

Some use structured interviews before entry to medical school. One group look for 'tolerance of ambiguity' [7], and I would agree with this. A patient once said to me, *'a few weeks ago I would like to have known if I had cancer and how serious it was, but now I think you'd be better not telling me'*. When quoting this to nurses or medical students, it is striking to watch their faces and to see how some are comfortable with it (smiling kindly at the unconscious humour and the rather charming ambivalence of it) while others just look puzzled, anxious or embarrassed. I know which kind I would like to have looking after me if I had advanced cancer.

How much of the problem is due to a sense of failure — failure to defeat death, especially cancer death? Or to an inability to accept our own mortality? It has been suggested (I have been unable to trace by whom) that doctors as a group are even more frightened of death than other people; and that this is partly why they decided to become doctors — to fight what they fear. If so, have we given enough thought to various ways of reducing this disabling fear?

Conclusion

In a 'hopeless' situation, tender loving care is not enough, concern and compassion are not enough. Somewhere along the road between old-fashioned TLC and new-fangled counselling, lies something as old as Medicine itself, which I have called here friendly professional interest. For the doctor — whatever else is said or done — FPI is the basic minimum. It need not take up a lot of time; and it does not need special training beyond what ought to be given in every Medical School. Lack of it is a common cause of low morale and misery.

Though many doctors have no problems of this kind and have always practiced excellent effortless FPI as part of their job, more thought needs to be given to why so many others, when the outlook is bad (especially if the cause is cancer) seem to find it difficult to be relaxed and friendly; difficult to be professional; and difficult to be interested, either in the patient or his symptoms.

References

1. Cartwright A, Hockey L, Anderson JL. Life before Death. London: Routledge & Kegan Paul, 1973

2. Maguire P, Fairbairn S, Fletcher C. Consultation skills of young doctors. *Br Med J* 1986; **292**: 1573–8

3. Saunders CM. Terminal care. In: *Oxford textbook of medicine.* Oxford: Oxford University Press, 1983: **26**.3–14

4. Baines M. Pain relief in active patients with cancer: analgesic drugs are the foundation of management. *Br Med J* 1989; **298**: 36–8

5. Hockley JM, Dunlop R, Davies RJ. Survey of distressing symptoms in dying patients and their families in hospital and the response to a symptom control team. *Br Med J* 1988; **296**: 1715–17

6. Brewin TB. The cancer patient: communication and morale. *Br Med J* 1977; **2**: 1623–7

7. Powis DA, Neame RLB, Bristow T, Murphy LB. The objective structured interview for medical student selection. *Br Med J* 1988; **296**: 765–8

To achieve a sense of proportion about small risks of any kind can be remarkably difficult, and nobody knows this better than those of us concerned with radiation risks. The best way for many people seems to be to remind them of the risks and uncertainty of many commonplace activities — e.g., a straightforward journey by road of, say, fifty miles under favourable conditions. Such travelling is neither dangerous (in the usual sense of the word) nor is it completely safe. Something may go wrong. Neither comfort nor safety can be guaranteed. Everyone knows this, yet nearly everyone is happy to make the journey. Purists will quibble over a crude analogy of this kind, but it does seem to help some people to understand the position in which a doctor often finds himself when asked if a procedure is 'completely safe'; and it might presumably make some sense in a court of law. At the very least, gross misconceptions are less likely.

(Extract from a letter to the Editor, *The Lancet* 1978 ii 1049–50)

The cancer patient – too many scans and x-rays?

Reprinted from
The Lancet,
1981, Vol ii, pages 1098–1099

A man with proven lung cancer, progressive weakness, and weight loss has a focal fit for the first time in his life. A brain scan is ordered. Why? The odds in favour of a brain metastasis are overwhelming — and remain so even if the scan is normal. So why spend precious money? Why use valuable resources of staff and equipment, sometimes an unexpectedly wide variety of them, including, for example, an ambulance and its crew, who are thus made unavailable for other duties? And even if money and resources are unlimited, why risk causing anxiety and discomfort?

Without in any way questioning their value in diagnosis, this paper seeks to discuss and to challenge the increasing use of post-diagnostic isotope scans, skeletal X-rays, ultrasonography, computed tomography, and the like (all to be referred to from now on simply as 'scans'), not only in advanced poor-prognosis situations such as the one cited, but also in apparently healthy patients with nothing clinically to suggest distant spread.

The best reason — some would say the only reason — for ordering a test is to modify management if the findings so indicate. At diagnosis it may be logical to search for distant spread and, if this is found, to modify or abandon plans for local therapy and to start systemic therapy. But quite often treatment is not modified.

One reason is that normal scans do not prove that dissemination has not occurred. Since a cubic millimetre of blood can contain several million red cells, clearly there is plenty of room for several hundred thousand cancer cells in a cubic millimetre of tissue. Since no scan can detect a lesion this small, it may sometimes be thought that chemotherapy (or hormone therapy) should be given anyway. On the other hand, the benefits of existing drugs (taking into consideration side-effects, including psychological disadvantages), may be considered insufficient to justify their use in the absence of symptoms; so once again scan findings may not have any effect on management. Finally, although local surgery or radiotherapy may be modified by 'positive' results, this is often not so. Apart from possible doubt about the findings (and the fact that in some situations, for example breast cancer, scans are sometimes not done until after surgery) it may be thought that the best way to achieve a good quality of life is to remove the primary growth and at the same time to take steps (either by removal of surrounding 'normal' tissue or by radiotherapy or by both) to make local recurrence as unlikely as possible. In other words, despite a positive finding, to do the same as would have been done if the scans had been normal.

The same sort of thing happens in follow-up clinics. A kind of letter that is increasingly being sent out first describes the finding of apparent rib metastases (from breast carcinoma) in a 'routine' bone scan; then records the decision to take no action in view of the total absence of any symptoms; and finally says that the scan will be repeated in two months. It is difficult to see how the patient benefits from these scans, which are not altering management; and which may merely cause anxiety and interfere with rehabilitation after removal of all clinically evident disease.

Suppose the finding of symptomless metastases does alter management. To say that treatment is now 'more logical' or 'more rational' is not enough. We have to ask a second question. How good is the evidence that such altered mangement has a favourable effect (a) in the short term (b) in the long term? Here there are many potential pitfalls. For example, just as earlier diagnosis automatically increases duration of survival after diagnosis, so more accurate staging (after scans have found unsuspected spread) may seem to improve results in certain stages, even if not a single patient is any better off. The prognosis of a group of stage 2 patients, for example, can hardly fail to benefit if cases previously called stage 1 are added to it and if some of its more advanced cases move to stage 3. When assessing the benefits of modern staging methods we need first to allow for such apparent — but, in fact, artificial — 'improvement'.

The best way of getting an answer would be to conduct randomised trials of the kind that recently examined the value of endoscopy after gastrointestinal bleeding.[1] If different cancer treatment policies can be randomised, so can different investigational policies. The ethical principles are the same. The problems should be no greater. If we are convinced that a scan is either indicated or contraindicated, then we must not randomise;

but whenever we are uncertain it would be ethical to do so. Otherwise, we run the risk of subjecting patients indefinitely to investigations of doubtful value, which could even turn out in the end to be doing more harm than good — either because few, if any, procedures are 100% safe, or because overinvestigation can easily lead to overtreatment, with its attendant risks.

Are scans justified purely to help with prognosis? In terms simply of information for patient or relative such justification must surely have only a low priority. Expensive tests should seldom be needed merely to reassure; and the conversion of a guarded prognosis to a gloomy one is far more likely to harm the quality of life than to help it. Except in rare cases, the idea that a patient needs to know that he has unsuspected metastases, so that he can *"put his affairs in order"*, is a very weak argument. Since anyone can die any day from a road accident or heart attack, affairs ought to have been settled anyway. It is true that in advanced cancer some decisions depend on whether the patient is likely to live for six weeks or six months, but here clinical assessment and a careful history (often obtained with the aid of a relative or nurse and taking special note of progressive weakness or loss of interest and the speed with which they are taking place) are generally far more helpful than anything a scan may show.

Finally, clinical research — to discover as much as possible about the natural history of a tumour and how it spreads; and, if a new method of imaging comes along, to assess its sensitivity, specificity, and relation to existing methods. When such studies are carefully and ethically done in a few centres and published without delay this is clearly money well spent. But when large numbers of scans are done routinely in numerous hospitals, with no more than a vague idea that something might one day be learnt from them, clinical research as a justification for scanning begins to look very thin.

To some, Richard Asher's blunt charge that *"overinvestigation is a form of physical cruelty"*[2] will seem an exaggeration. But in speaking of "safe, easy, non-invasive investigation" it must be remembered that some patients have a low threshold for discomfort, anxiety, or both; and that others, previously stoical may change when they grow old or in the course of a long illness, so that even a simple injection is dreaded, to say nothing of a long wait in a hospital corridor or 10 minutes lying on a rock-hard X-ray table, body aching, mouth dry, wondering what is going to happen next.

And here lies another point seldom considered. Patients who have found their investigations an ordeal will talk to their friends and neighbours. *"You have to be fit to be in hospital these days"* is a comment I've overheard. If we do not reduce the number of tests done to the essential minimum, we may easily encourage the very thing we ought to be trying to reduce — fear of hospitals — a fear which already leads to much delay and often (quite apart from the possibility of missing a chance of cure) to months of avoidable suffering and loss of social life. "*If I had known how easy it could be*", said one patient whose investigations had been kept to an absolute minimum, "*I would have come long ago*".

Many investigations which can hardly be called vital, can nevertheless not be proved as unnecessary. In this large grey area, clinical judgement is as important as it is in decisions regarding treatment. Ideally, investigations that carry a low priority (because they are unlikely to have any important effect on management) should be recognised as such and seldom done — partly out of consideration for the patient (who trusts us not to order scans unless they are necessary) and partly with an eye on the welfare of other patients (present and future) who trust us to have sensible priorities.

Unfortunately, many pressures work in the opposite direction and their combined force can be surprisingly difficult to resist. It is never easy — and may even be thought ostentatious or eccentric — to swim too strongly against the tide of medical fashion. No doctor wants to appear out of touch with modern practice; and scan findings can add to the interest of our work. Martin *et al*[3] were able, by discussion with medical residents, to achieve a 47% reduction in laboratory tests, but they had no significant success with radiological investigations. Too often (partly for defensive, legalistic reasons) the motto seems to be "*if in doubt, do it*", whereas it should be "*if in doubt, don't*" — at least not until the need for it has been discussed.

Polyscannery like polypharmacy, is a highly infectious condition. If we are not careful, we shall slowly drift into a situation where many post-diagnostic scans become, at best, an expensive placebo, a vaguely comforting pseudoscientific ritual; at worst, an unnecessary ordeal for patients and a betrayal of their trust in us.

Perhaps, before nuclear magnetic resonance and other advances place still further temptations in our path, we should spend a little more time discussing the principles involved. The greater the availability of the latest technology, the greater the danger that what is revealed becomes an end in itself. "*After all*", said a young doctor anxious to order several scans for an elderly patient, yet admitting that they would be unlikely to alter management, "*this is supposed to be a teaching hospital*". Exactly. So what should we teach? What example should we be setting? Overinvestigation? Or clinical judgment?

References

1. Peterson WL, Barnett CC, Smith HJ, Alen MH, Corbett DB. Routine early endoscopy in upper gastro-intestinal tract bleeding. 1981 *New Engl J Med;* **304:** 925.

2. Asher R. The seven sins of medicine. 1949 *Lancet;* **ii:** 358.

3. Martin AR, Wolf MA, Thibodeau LA, Dzau V, Braunwald E. A trial of two strategies to modify the test-ordering behaviour of medical residents. 1980 *New Engl J Med;* **303:** 1330.

SIR —

This apparent contradiction — more money spent on the NHS than ever before, yet cuts in services — is easily explained if we find that we are now spending a lot more money per patient seen or treated. Are we? If so, how much of it is justified?[1-3] For example, how many investigations are very unlikely to alter management? Given the fact that more money spent on one thing means less for something else, should we be doing them?[4-6]

1. Editorial. Pathology tests. Too much of a good thing. *Lancet;* 1984; **i:** 1278.

2. Reuben DB. Learning diagnostic restraint. *New Engl J Med;* 1984; **310:** 591–593.

3. Editorial. Taming high technology. *B Ara Med J;* 1984; **289:** 393–394.

4. Editorial. Expensive medical techniques. *Lancet;* 1983; **i:** 279–280.

5. Brewin TB. The cancer patient: too many scans and x-rays? *Lancet;* 1981; **ii:** 1098–1099.

6. Hardison JE. To be complete. *New Engl J Med;* 1979; **300:** 193–194.

(Letter to the Editor, *The Lancet;* 1986; **i:** 1502)

Principles of
radiotherapy

Reprinted from
Cancer in the Elderly, 1990, Chapter 5,
Eds: Caird & Brewin, pubs: Wright, London

Some general remarks about the history and basic principles of radiotherapy are relevant, since this is a subject that is often poorly understood outside radiotherapy departments. Without some insight into it, the various ways in which elderly cancer patients can be helped will be less clear.

By one of those coincidences that occur from time to time in the history of medicine and science, X-rays were discovered in 1895 and radioactivity (the natural radiation coming from parts of the earth's crust) 2 years later. Both were soon tried as treatment for tumours. Even in those early days, they were seen to be more effective (at least on the surface) than the electrical therapy previously employed by a few enthusiasts (Macintyre, 1891, 1903).

X-rays are produced by an electrical machine. Switch off the electricity and all radiation ceases. Radioactivity, whether natural or artificial, cannot be switched off; it can only be shielded until it is decided to let some of it escape in a precisely timed and controlled way.

Some principles and options

Radiation dosage can be confusing. Because of all the modifying factors it is unwise to quote doses without consulting a radiotherapy colleague. The concept is quite different from that of drug dosage (Brewin 1977). The total amount of radiation directed at the patient is not normally recorded. What is recorded is something much more relevant — the concentration achieved in the target area (or at any other point of interest). The only reason that such 'doses' are recorded in radiotherapy, but not in drug therapy, is that only in the case of radiation can they be accurately calculated. With drugs there are too many unknown factors (absorption, clearance, the permeability of membranes and so on). It follows that radiation doses to different areas cannot be added together to give a total dose of radiation received by the patient. To do so is as meaningless as it would be to add together the population densities (number of people per square mile) of two different towns.

Another source of confusion depends on biology, not physics. The overall time and the number of exposures ('fractions') needs to be stated. From the point of view of biological effect 5000 cGy (rads) in 6 weeks, with treatments 5 times a week, is not as high a dose as 4000 cGy in 3 weeks, with treatments twice a week.

In the treatment of cancer, either an X-ray unit or a radioactive source can be used to produce a beam of radiation. This beam can be as wide or as narrow as desired. In the earliest days of radiotherapy it was not understood why it could heal skin cancer, but 'hopelessly failed' (as one pioneer frankly expressed it) when directed at deep-seated tumours. Later it was realized that each beam loses energy as it enters the body (very rapidly in the case of the early low-energy radiation). Complicated 'cross-fire' techniques were devised with as many as five or six beams coming in from different directions and converging on the tumour. Then more powerful radiation became available; more advanced X-ray units (usually linear accelerators) and, along with nuclear power, many kinds of artificial radioactivity (cobalt, caesium and so on). More energy meant better penetration, and much shorter treatment times than were given by the early X-ray units or the radium discovered by Marie Curie. The new radiation was not only more powerful; it was gentler, too. The maximum dose from each beam was no longer on the surface (where it was likely to lead to soreness and redness of the skin similar to sunburn), but just below it. So, provided that there was no reason to think there might be cancer cells in the skin, a 'skin-sparing' technique could now be used. Unfortunately, however, there is no similar way of sparing internal epithelium; so local radiation reactions affecting the mucous membranes at such sites as the mouth, oesophagus, bladder and rectum, can still cause great discomfort for a week or more, but only if a high dose has to be directed at them.

Another advantage of these more powerful radiations was fewer cases of nausea or vomiting (probably because of less unwanted radiation scattered outside each beam). Many radiotherapy patients are now quite free from such side-effects, especially if given appropriate explanation, reassurance and encouragement (nausea being sometimes more a symptom of fear than of radiation). But with some, the problem remains.

Since the early days of radiotherapy, methods other than beam therapy have also been used. Radioactive sources — needles, tubes, etc. — can be inserted into the tumour or placed in contact with it, for instance radioactive needles in the tongue; not as brutal as it sounds, and successful in curing many cases of carcinoma, when the only alternative is excision of a large part of the tongue. Insertion of radioactive sources into the uterus and vagina has cured thousands of women with cancer at these sites, without the need for surgery. Later, when artificial radioactivity became available, radioactive liquids were either injected intravenously (iodine, with selective uptake in the thyroid gland; phosphorus, and so on) or instilled into the bladder or other body cavities.

At one time it was thought that one kind of radiotherapy was best for one kind of cancer and one for another. But it is now generally agreed that the biological effect of all these ionizing radiations is the same. The only reason to prefer one to the other is their physical properties. These affect their penetrating power, the time taken to give the dose, the need for a general anaesthetic, cost, convenience, and so on.

Not cautery, but a differential effect

Radiotherapy is not cautery. The tumour is not 'destroyed, with careful avoidance of the surrounding normal tissue'. This is a popular misconception. If that is all it was, it would be much cheaper to give an anaesthetic and then use electrocoagulation or some other kind of cautery. To sterilize food that may contain anaerobic bacteria requires a single exposure of 5 megarads (Lancet 1970) — **1000 times** the sort of dose that would be regarded as dangerously high in radiotherapy. It would be more true to say that radiation has remarkable healing properties, the dose required varying with different kinds of cancer. A low dose rapidly shrinks some tumours, for example, lymphoma, seminoma, small cell lung cancer and many childhood tumours. Others need much more.

Normal tissues can be damaged, too, some much more easily than others. As with malignant tissue, a dose of radiation that is unlikely to have any effect on one kind of tissue may harm another. Whether the effect is transient or permanent depends on the dose. The function of a cell (whose normal job is to produce, say, mucus or saliva) may cease for a few weeks and then, if the dose is not too high, recover completely. The important point is that the optimum dose (which will depend on a number of factors) can often eradicate the tumour without any serious effect on normal tissue (which may, for reasons discussed later, have been deliberately radiated to the same dose as the tumour).

The explanation for this differential effect is poorly understood. It is certainly not just a matter of cancer cells dividing more rapidly than normal ones, nor does it depend on cell differentiation (Hall 1973). Many highly differentiated squamous carcinomas are cured by radiotherapy. Despite more than 80 years of study, there seems to be something basic that eludes us, perhaps something that is common to the mechanism of both radiotherapy and cancer chemotherapy.

Radiotherapy is more versatile than either surgery or chemotherapy. The surgeon has to decide how much to remove, the chemotherapist what dose to give. With radiotherapy, on the other hand, there first has to be a decision as to how much of the body to expose to radiation (a decision that in the case of local radiotherapy, intended to cure, corresponds to the surgeon's decision); and next there has to be a decision as to what dose to give.

Why does the surgeon (except in the case of benign tumours) deliberately excise apparently normal tissue around the tumour? Why does the radiation oncologist carefully give to such tissue a high dose of radiation? Because in both cases there may be hidden cancer cells. There is plenty of room in a cubic **millimetre** of tissue for a million cancer cells, so no test is sensitive enough to ensure normality. Surgeon and radiotherapist each have to make an intelligent guess, based on known patterns of spread, balanced by the harm that might result from too radical an approach.

When radiotherapy is given to the whole body the effect is similar to giving chemotherapy. And here we come to a fundamental problem. For various reasons (the marked radiosensitivity of blood cell formation in the bone marrow being one) the more of the body that is exposed to radiation, the smaller the dose that can safely be given. This explains why widespread disease can often not be adequately treated, compared with more localized disease of the same radiosensitivity. It is the advent of widespread disease, not increasing radioresistance, that is the usual reason why radiation may no longer have anything to offer except treatment of selected parts of the cancer (usually those parts causing symptoms).

So-called radioresistant tumours

Is there any kind of cancer not affected by radiotherapy? *'Usually regarded as radioresistant'* is the popular textbook phrase; and this is thought to mean that surgery or chemotherapy is preferable, or that radiotherapy is not even worth trying. But nobody has ever published a series of, say, 20 or 30 consecutive cases of any kind of localized 'radio-resistant' cancer, showing no responses when all were given a conventional high dose of radiation. On the contrary, such a dose, say the highest dose that can be given with reasonable safety to a volume not exceeding 8–10cm in diameter, is likely to be completely ineffective in only about a third of cases. Another third will show partial regression, which may bring complete relief of symptoms, and perhaps a long remission if the tumour is slow growing. Another third will show complete regression, permanent in many cases. This striking variation is seen within each tumour type and, like the average radiosensitivity of different tumour types, cannot be predicted from the histology (Friedman 1975). More reliable is the clinical observation that when tumours are bulky, fixed and very firm they are less likely to respond.

This rough order of response applies, for example, to fibrosarcoma (Windeyer, Dische and Mansfield 1966; Suit, Russell and Martin 1975), malignant melanoma (Khan and Ross 1984; Ellis 1984), and certain salivary tumours (Rafla 1982; Henk 1986). Surgery (perhaps combined with radiotherapy) seems to be best for them, so long as the disease remains localized and there is no contraindication. But surgery, too, may fail; and because of the probability of selection bias, and the lack of randomized comparisons, it is hard to be sure. Finally, if surgery is considered impossible or unwise, it is important to know that there is at present no kind of cancer, whatever its reputation for radioresistance, where a useful and lasting local response is more likely with chemotherapy than with radiotherapy.

So we ought to say, not 'radioresistant', but 'how radioresistant'? Better still, forget the misleading word 'radioresistant' and just ask, 'how radiosensitive'? And, for the future, it is no good improving the radiosensitivity of cancer cells unless there is an improvement in the ratio between the effect on cancer cells and on normal cells. A drug that actually made cancer cells more resistant to radiation would still be an advance, if there was an even greater increase in the resistance of normal cells. This 'therapeutic ratio' principle, recognized by radiotherapists over half a century ago (Paterson 1948) is equally true of cancer chemotherapy. It must be, if the effect on cancer cells and the effect on normal cells are both dose dependent.

Cure, remission and palliation

Most people now realize that cancer is not always incurable. But there is still a reluctance to recognize that many cases are cured by radiation alone. Some of these are operable (e.g. carcinoma of larynx, mouth, cervix, or skin) and could have had surgery. But with certain cancers, radiotherapy cure rates seem to be as good as surgical ones. So a choice has to be made on the basis of comparative morbidity, risk (early and late), loss of function, patient preference, availability, convenience, and so on. The advice given will often follow discussion between different specialists, each carefully considering what seems best in all the circumstances for the particular patient they are discussing.

In this situation some elderly patients will wish to have a lot of information about each method of treatment (even including the very serious remote risks of each); others, not wanting to hear all the details, will have a definite preference for one or the other; while others prefer just to trust professional advice. It must also be remembered that if radiotherapy is chosen and then fails, surgery may still be possible, and may achieve cure (for example, in carcinoma of the larynx), though in certain sites there may be increased surgical morbidity after a high dose of radiation.

Many inoperable tumours, too, may still have a chance of long remission — or even cure — following radiotherapy. It is strange that not only the public and the media, but even some doctors and nurses, still talk as if an inoperable malignant tumour means that the patient has not got long to live. It may be so, but often it is not.

Finally, radiotherapy is of great value in advanced cancer. Its value lies in its ability to relieve symptoms; not systemic symptoms like weakness, anorexia, nausea, or generalized discomfort (which it is unlikely to help unless widespread disease is so radiosensitive that quite low doses are effective) but local symptoms, in particular pain, pressure symptoms of various kinds, malignant ulceration, and bleeding. Such symptoms can often be partially or totally relieved with few or no side-effects, provided the patient's attitude and tolerance are correctly assessed, and not too much is attempted.

Pain
When pain is due to pressure on a nerve from a soft tissue mass, a small reduction in tumour size may completely relieve the pain. Pain due to direct invasion of bone by a primary growth responds less well. But pain from a blood-borne bone metastasis will nearly always respond, whatever the histology or site of the primary. This is one of the most valuable uses of radiotherapy.

In each case the radiotherapist must assess the origin of the pain on clinical evidence (it may be a referred pain, it may not), and not just 'treat the X-rays'. The area that looks the worst may not be causing the pain. Shrewd clinical judgement is also needed when deciding how much, if anything, to do in the way of prophylactic radiation to prevent possible future pain or fracture from deposits (or possible deposits) not at present causing symptoms.

If it is not going to upset the patient or do any harm, generous amounts of adjacent normal-looking tissue that might easily contain occult metastases are often best irradiated. For example, a metastasis in a long bone usually calls for radiation of the whole shaft, and a brain metastasis for radiation of the whole brain (which makes precise pretreatment localization techniques an unnecessary and time-consuming refinement for any patient, but particularly for an elderly one). But in the case of incurable abdominal cancer (for example recurrent rectal carcinoma causing perineal pain and difficulty in sitting comfortably), it is often wiser just to concentrate on those areas causing symptoms, using a single 'skin sparing' beam; otherwise diarrhoea (due to loops of bowel in the high dose region), nausea, or weakness may outweigh benefit, and the elderly patient and his family may wish the treatment had never been given.

Pressure and obstruction
Since the body is full of soft tubes, carrying blood, lymph, air, food, urine or faeces, it is clear that a tumour growing in the lumen or pressing from the outside can cause a partial or complete blockage, with predictable symptoms according to site and function. Tumour shrinkage will often restore normal function and give welcome relief of symptoms. Common examples are a swollen face and neck due to superior vena caval block, shortness of breath due to bronchial obstruction, oedema of an arm or leg due to enlarged lymph nodes, and dysphagia due to a tumour affecting the mouth, throat or oesophagus.

A less common but important syndrome occurs in elderly women when a rapidly growing and aggressively invasive thyroid tumour presses on the trachea. The histology may suggest either lymphoma or anaplastic carcinoma. Whichever it is, it is vital to ask not just how long the swelling has been present but what size it was a week or so ago. And if there is a short history of rapid growth, the response to quite a small dose of radiation is usually dramatic. Such treatment is urgent, and often relieves pressure on the trachea within hours. Excision in these cases is never complete; and minimal surgery, without any tracheostomy, is probably better than attempts to excise as much of the tumour as possible. Unfortunately, however, whatever is done there are not in this situation many 5-year survivors, most patients dying within a year or two, often of lung metastases.

Bleeding and ulceration

For some reason this useful effect of radiation in advanced cancer is often not mentioned in medical or surgical textbooks. Whenever the cause is malignant ulceration, quite a moderate dose of radiation will often reduce or abolish haemoptysis, haematuria, uterine bleeding and so on. This will have both physical and psychological benefits. If there is a fungating tumour, for example of the breast (no matter how much secondary infection there is, and no matter how long it has been present), partial or complete healing is normally achieved, with a reduction in odour and discharge and an improvement in secondary infection. The fear that radiation may make such a necrotic area even worse is largely misplaced. It is very unusual for this to occur.

Difficult decisions

In deciding whether to give palliative radiotherapy to an elderly patient, sound clinical judgment is vital. Whether such judgement can be taught or is an inborn faculty has been debated (Hutchison 1928). The careful weighing of pros and cons is certainly helped by experience, imagination and empathy. There must be a clear objective, stated in terms of symptom relief (less pain, for example, or better sleep, or easier breathing, or an end to bleeding from the tumour). And there must be a reasonable expectation that the price paid, in terms of side-effects and inconvenience, will be such that the patient will be glad that he had the treatment. Unless various factors are carefully assessed, it is easy to do more harm than good. Two factors are especially important:

1. *Prognosis* — The most serious mistake is to inflict anxiety and discomfort (worse still, radiation side-effects) on an elderly patient whose general condition is deteriorating, who probably has only a few weeks or less to live, and whose symptoms would be better treated in other ways. To avoid this, clinical acumen is more reliable than biochemistry or scans. Perhaps the most useful tip is to recognize extreme weakness of the kind that so often means that death is not far away, and which itself will make any travelling for treatment (even within a hospital) an ordeal. When seeing a patient for the first time it is especially vital to have a word with a nurse or close relative. How is the patient compared with a week ago? Is she getting rapidly weaker?

On the other hand almost equally bad is when the opinion of a radiotherapist is not requested because of a mistaken idea that the patient is unlikely to live more than a short time. This is often because scans show widespread metastases, and it is assumed that at this stage all types of cancer, regardless of the clinical picture, have the same prognosis. This may mean that an elderly patient, who could be helped by radiotherapy, is not given it.

2. *Attitude of the patient* — Nothing could be worse than to treat all elderly cancer patients alike, and to base what is done merely on age, diagnosis and extent of disease. The patient's attitude to different kinds of treatment is important. So is her tolerance of symptoms of various kinds, and her priorities, such as her attitude to survival. Prolongation of life may be the last thing she wants, and she may have to be tactfully reassured that the sole purpose of what is proposed is symptom relief. On the other hand, she may want to live a little longer for some special reason, such as to see a grandchild graduate or marry.

Simplicity and flexibility

In spite of pressure of work and complaints of insufficient resources, radiation oncologists, like so many other hospital doctors, seem to be tempted to over-investigate and to introduce expensive or time-consuming treatment refinements, when something simpler would be more appropriate. Reasons for this are not hard to find. They probably include the following:

1. Wanting each patient, however old, to be impressed with modern technology and to feel that he is getting 'first class' treatment.

2. A fear of errors if the team treating the patient does not go through 'standard' procedures with every patient.

3. Real or imagined medicolegal and 'defensive' considerations.

4. Staff interest in technological advances.

But many elderly patients, especially if in pain or feeling unwell, will warmly welcome some statement such as:
'I've got some good news for you, you don't need any special measuring, checks or scans this time; we are going to get straight on with the treatment, a single beam of radiation is all we need — it will take only a few minutes — and then you will be able to get back to your bed.'

Maximum flexibility in regard to the timing of treatment will also be appreciated by the elderly patient and will help her morale and quality of life. The frequency of visits and the overall time of a course of treatment can both be adjusted to suit various circumstances, such as dislike of travelling (especially by ambulance), domestic problems, special occasions that the patient would be sorry to miss, likely tolerance of large 'fractions' of radiation and so on. Appropriate dose adjustments must be made and special care taken to be sure that there is no error due to departure from a 'standard' schedule. But, even in the busiest unit, it is sad to be so fearful of possible error or confusion that all flexibility is lost. This is not the way to get the greatest benefit (and the least anxiety and inconvenience to the patient) from palliative radiotherapy.

Sometimes the elderly patient and the doctor will decide together on just one attendance a week for a number of weeks, allowing time to modify the treatment if reactions develop. Sometimes there will be good reasons (medical or just patient preference) to get it all over within a few days. For relieving pain from bone metastases, a single exposure may be enough (Bates 1987); certainly more than a very few visits for this purpose is unnecessary.

When a higher dose has to be given, daily treatments (Monday to Friday), maybe for several weeks, are quite often a strain for elderly outpatients. Attendance two or three times a week is much easier. A day's rest after a trying day is a great boon. But how often this is appropriate is a matter of controversy among radiotherapists. Certainly, when skin cancer affects the distal arm or leg of an elderly patient with poor peripheral circulation there is an increased risk of radionecrotic ulceration. This seems to be reduced if the dose is divided into a fairly large number of small fractions.

Another reason for flexibility (as with chemotherapy) is whenever side-effects seem to be outweighing benefit. This may call for very fine judgement, based on all kinds of considerations that must be given different weight for each individual patient. Sometimes it will be best to put all the pros and cons frankly to the patient. Sometimes to do so will merely add to her distress, giving her only a choice of options that are each calculated to fill her with fear and depression. No two cases are exactly the same.

There are three further points about flexibility. First, it must be remembered that to advise stopping the treatment or reducing the dose will be welcome news to some patients, but that others will feel depressed and abandoned if their mood is wrongly assessed and the reasons given insensitively. Secondly, for an elderly patient with advanced cancer to be described as 'refusing further treatment' suggests something wrong with the doctor-patient relationship. Mutual agreement to stop, based partly on how the patient feels, should be the norm. Thirdly, it is important to tell the patient and his family **in advance** that a flexible approach will be taken and that it is not possible to say how long the course of treatment will last. If this is not done, there is a risk that either the patient or one of his relatives will feel that she lacks stoicism, and that this has led to premature stopping of the treatment.

Too much or too little

A balance must be struck between doing too much or too little. An example of the former was when an 80-year-old man attended a medical outpatient department for over a year with large lymphoid masses on both sides of his neck and a large undifferentiated primary tumour in his nasopharynx. He had no pain and no serious difficulty in breathing or swallowing, and it was assumed that radiotherapy would be a great ordeal for him at his age and make his throat sore. When a modest dose of radiation caused all the masses to regress completely within 10 days, restoring normal comfort and appearance, with minimal side-effects, he naturally wondered why he hadn't been offered this treatment sooner.

Another elderly patient had paraplegia due to spinal cord compression. Biopsy had shown myeloma and it had been wrongly assumed that radiotherapy would be futile, so he was transferred for terminal care, bedridden, on morphine for his pain and with an indwelling catheter. Radiotherapy, even at this late stage (as is not uncommon when myeloma causes spinal cord compression) had an almost immediate and dramatic effect. He lost his pain, recovered full bladder function, and after several weeks' physiotherapy and encouragement was able to walk again and remained active for several more years.

Sometimes the spouse or family of an elderly cancer patient, especially if the chance of cure is slim, will not want radiotherapy to be given. This is likely to be due to fears that it will be distressing. that it will be ineffective, or that it is intended merely to try to prolong life. The use of radiotherapy purely to relieve pain and other symptoms (in an easy, gentle way, without upsetting the patient) is hardly ever mentioned by writers and journalists, since it does not fit in with popular misconceptions about cancer and about radiation. So public confusion is not surprising. The only answer is to explain carefully the object of the treatment and the likely side-effects, and to stress that the doctor is only proposing what he would want for himself or his own family.

Conclusion

Radiotherapy by itself (without any need for admission to hospital, anaesthetic, or surgery) can cure some of the cancers that affect the elderly, with tolerable side-effects. In other cases surgery or chemotherapy will be the mainstay of treatment but radiation will be useful as an adjuvant. In advanced cancer a good radiotherapist ('good' always implying sound judgement as well as careful technique) will either firmly advise against radiotherapy, for one of the reasons mentioned in this chapter, or will take full advantage of its versatility and flexibility to give the elderly patient maximum help, combined with minimum anxiety, side effects and inconvenience.

References

Bates, T. (1987) *Palliative Medicine,* **1**. 117

Brewin, T.B. (1977) *Br. J. Radiol.,* **50**. 430

Ellis, F. (1984) *Br. J. Radiol.,* **57**. 1044

Friedman, M. (1975) *Br. J. Radiol.,* **48**. 81

Hall, E.J. (1973) *Radiobiology for the Radiologist,* Harper & Row, New York

Henk, J.M. (1986) In *Radiotherapy in Clinical Practice* (ed. H.F. Hope-Stone), Butterworths, London, p. 93

Hutchison, R. (1928) *Br. Med. J.,* **i**. 335

Khan, M.S. and Ross, W.M. (1984) *Clin. Radiol.,* **35**. 151

Lancet (1970) *Lancet,* **ii**. 1024

Macintyre, J. (1891) *J. Laryngol.,* **5**. 39

Macintyre, J. (1903) *Br. Med. J.,* **ii**. 199

Paterson, R. (1948) *The Treatment of Malignant Disease by Radiotherapy,* Edward Arnold, London

Rafla, S. (1982) In *Treatment of Cancer* (ed. K.E. Halnan), Chapman & Hall, London, p. 269

Suit, H.D., Russell, W.O. and Martin, R.G. (1975) *Cancer* **35**, 1478

Windeyer, B., Dische, S. and Mansfield, C.M. (1966) *Clin. Radiol.,* **17**, 32

Need for a common language?

Reprinted from
Clinical Oncology,
1993, Vol 5, page 277

'*Recent evidence suggests that radiotherapy is definitely active in this type of cancer.*'

'*In chemotherapy the incidence of side effects is related, not only to the total dose, but to fractionation and overall time.*'

'*This tumour has been generally regarded as radio-resistant, but new radiotherapy techniques have achieved partial response rates of 60%–70% and complete response rates of 15%–20%.*'

'*This condition is generally regarded as chemo-resistant, so other forms of treatment are indicated.*'

What do these four statements have in common? Why do they all sound a little strange? Nobody is offering a free weekend break to the sender of the first correct answer received, but astute readers may already have suspected that, in the style of Richard Asher[1], I have not quoted real statements, but invented some in order to make a point. When speaking of radiotherapy I have used language from the world of chemotherapy. When mentioning chemotherapy I have used phrases that we have become accustomed to think of only in connection with radiotherapy.

Often there seems to be no real need for expressing in two ways (according to whether the treatment is radiotherapy or chemotherapy) what is basically the same thing. Whenever appropriate, why do not we use a common language? It might help understanding. Each therapy could give up one or more of its pet phrases, and a single phrase be shared by both.

Similarly, why should not the words 'concentrated' and 'dilute' be shared by both the world of chemistry and the world of physics? Why don't we refer to dilute radiation, just as we do to dilute solutions? Concentration and dilution are concepts that every one understands. Might this not help health professions to understand better the nature of radiation and its dosage, and the public to get into better proportion the remote risks of exposure to small amounts of it?

The reason that radiotherapy and chemotherapy have fundamentally different concepts of dose is simple, but how many not trained in radiation understand it? How often do those of us trained to use radiation explain to others that, after a patient has taken a drug, no matter by what route, we cannot measure its concentration in different organs (if we could, we would, for that would be far more relevant than the total amount administered), whereas with radiation it is easy to do so? In the case of radiation it is a local concentration that we record: the amount per gram in the target volume, or whatever part of the body we choose to assess.

The classical radiotherapeutic concept of the therapeutic ratio[2] is another principle that ought to be a firm part of a common language. It is just as true of most, if not all, effective cancer chemotherapy as it is of radiotherapy. In fact, it cannot fail to be true of any form of therapy where the benefit and side effects are both dose dependent, and where it is fear of an unacceptable incidence of one or more serious side effects that stops a higher dose being given.

Flowing logically and inevitably from this principle is the interesting and vital fact — still not sufficiently appreciated by those just hoping for some way of improving the radiosensitivity or chemosensitivity of cancer cells — that an agent that made them less sensitive, not more sensitive, would be a great advance if, at the same time, normal cells showed an even greater shift towards resistance. Then the ratio would improve, and that is the only thing that counts.

There is nothing new about any of this, but perhaps we are not as good at explaining it to others as we should be; maybe it helps if each specialty shares words and phrases with others, and has as little of its own jargon as possible.

Incidentally, in relation to this problem of some cancer cells being 'resistant' to radiotherapy or chemotherapy, it is maybe worth bearing in mind that nobody is likely to regard the few soldiers or civilians who survive an intense bombardment as in some way bomb resistant.

References

1.   Jones FA, editor. Richard Asher talking sense. London: Pitman, 1972.

2.   Paterson R. The treatment of malignant disease by radiotherapy. London: Edward Arnold, 1948.

Excessive fear of dilute radiation

Reprinted from
the Journal of the Royal Society of Medicine,
1992, Vol 85, pages 311–313

There might be less misunderstanding of the dangers of radiation (especially after a nuclear accident or nuclear explosion) if we talked of how concentrated or how dilute the radiation is when it reaches an individual exposed to it; and if we applied to radiation more of the basic common sense that we apply to other risks. Excessive fear of dilute radiation can cause much needless mental anguish. In addition, if excessive fears could be reduced, evacuation policy in any future emergency could be much less drastic than that which has caused so much personal and economic hardship in the former USSR since the Chernobyl accident.

To talk of radiation being diluted as it spreads out from its origin (or as radioactive material widely dispersed) forms no part of standard terminology. The word 'dilute' traditionally belongs more to chemistry than to physics. But I believe that applying it to radiation would be appropriate and would contribute to public and professional understanding[1]. After all, for many years the essential difference between clinical radiation dosage and drug dosage has been that a radiation dose is expressed in terms of concentration. A rad (or its newer equivalent the centigray) represents not an amount but a concentration per gram. No doubt drug dosage would be expressed in the same way if, instead of relying on just the amount of the drug administered, we could easily and accurately measure its concentration in different tissues — as we can in the case of radiation[2].

Because of rapid dilution, the dose only a short distance from a dangerously high dose of radiation may be quite low and carry a surprisingly small risk. When there is an escape of radiation or of radioactive substances (as happened in the Chernobyl accident) the wider the area affected the greater is likely to be the dilution — and therefore the less the risk to the individual.

Misconceptions about the dangers of dilute radiation seem now to be quite common, even among normally well-informed people. In recent years almost the entire media have found that sensationalism, with emphasis on the more frightening or pessimistic aspects of each incident or official report, is popular and good for business. In a sense this misinformation is self-inflicted. Many people, it seems, though they like a doctor or nurse to reassure them, prefer a newspaper or television programme to frighten them. Masked faces, radiation danger signs, high wire fences, abandoned buildings and clicking Geiger counters (with suitable background music borrowed from horror movies) make good television.

For some years, along with a dramatic improvement in health and a better informed public, there has been increased anxiety about health[3]. "*Self torment through our obsession with health*" is how Taylor puts it[4].

One aspect of this is great concern about certain selected risks, even when the risk is very small — certain kinds of non-medical radiation being a prime example[5-7]. In the 1950s and 1960s consumer organisations and the media usually made a good job of explaining the dangers of radiation without exaggerating them[8]. Then there was a steady slide into misleading reporting. This became even worse after Chernobyl.

Many now seem to believe, for example, that the soil in the Chernobyl region was so heavily radiated that nothing will grow; that trees and vegetation were destroyed; that many animals died — cattle in the Ukraine, reindeer in Lapland, birds after flying through 'deadly clouds' of radiation, and so on; that thousands of the local population are suffering from various kinds of ill health directly caused by radiation; that every individual in certain regions runs a high risk of developing a radiation-induced cancer; that there has been an increase in the number of abnormal births, both animal and human; and that plant life, too, is showing genetic effects. Seldom before in this century, at least in peace time, have so many people been so misled.

Two new independent reports (by the Watt Committee on Energy[9] and by the International Atomic Energy Agency[10]) confirm the previous opinion of the World Health Organisation and of a combined Red Cross and Red Crescent team[10] that there is no good evidence that the health of the local population has been affected by radiation. When a comparison is made between people in the 'contaminated' zones and in other zones no differences have been found, other than anxiety. This is no surprise to anyone with a knowledge of the sort of concentrated doses that are truly dangerous and the sort of dilute doses that carry only a small or negligible risk. It is only what would be expected.

As for genetic birth defects these can be found in any community anywhere in the world, so it is easy for the media to find them and photograph them, but — so far at least — they have not become any more common. And, once again, this is no surprise, since (in spite of fears based on laboratory experiments) no increase has been seen in Japan since the nuclear bombs dropped 46 years ago[11], nor in the children of cancer patients after successful radiotherapy[12].

All those who, for one reason or another (medical or non-medical, intentional or accidental) absorb small amounts of extra radiation in the course of their life — extra, that is, to natural background radiation — have a right to know the truth about their chances of developing cancer many years later as a result. And the truth is that it will make little or no difference to whether they do or whether they don't. Cancer is a common disease; any difference there is will be very slight. Bearing in mind all the other risks in life[13] the best advice for the individual is to forget it. This advice is fully consistent with even the most pessimistic of reputable estimates. But it is seldom expressed in that way in the media. To do so would spoil the story — especially the Chernobyl story — by taking away much of the horror and drama. If there is widespread exposure to dilute radiation, the increased risk to the individual man or woman may be negligible — far less numerically than it is for many routine risks of travel and daily living that most people accept without any undue anxiety. But this risk — negligible for each individual — can be made to sound a matter of great concern simply by translating it into the total number of extra cancer cases that may occur in the future. If, when this is done, the first number that comes up doesn't look very impressive, it is easy for a journalist to continue to increase either the time scale or the total population covered — or both — until a sufficiently alarming figure is reached.

Unlike many new chemicals, all the main dangers of radiation were learned early in this century among those using it in hospital for diagnosis or treatment. Limits were set and for at least 60 years this has been a very safe occupation[14], which it wasn't before. This is in spite of an exposure that, at least until recently, was far in excess of that which now alarms the public.

In the very early days it was recognised that radiation could cause cancer as well as cure it. So far as dilute radiation is concerned, "*makes cancer in later life slightly more likely*" gives a truer impression than "*causes it*". Is this really so sinister? Water can save a man's life or drown him. Thousands of useful substances can cause cancer in certain conditions, in animals if not in humans. What about the absence of any safe threshold dose? Once again, far from being a specific and frightening feature of radiation, isn't this too quite commonplace? Driving a car a short distance obviously carries less risk than driving a long distance, but nobody asks for an official statement about the maximum safe distance.

How many of the public appreciate that every 'maximum permissible dose' of radiation (there is more than one, depending on the circumstances) is just an arbitrary point on a gradient? If we did the same for cigarettes and set a limit, we would not know whether to set it at one a year, or one a month, or one a week. If we fixed it at one a year, then just one cigarette a week would be *"more than 50 times the safe dose"*. The same applies to restrictions on the sale of meat or milk in areas exposed to dilute radiation. A much higher level of radioactivity than some very strict maximum may still be very safe, so far as the individual is concerned.

Radiation is so easy to measure (that's part of the trouble) that a dose that is 10 times as big as a very small dose (even 100 times as big) may still be a very small dose, still unlikely to do any harm. A Becquerel is a unit of radioactivity representing the disintegration of one atom per second. After the Chernobyl accident 200 Becquerels of radioactive iodine per litre of milk were found in some UK samples. This was alarming to those who didn't know that for more than 40 years many thousands of men and women with overactive thyroid glands have been given a million times this much radioactive iodine in a single dose (200 megaBecquerels or more). This treatment has been found to be very safe. The incidence of thyroid cancer, for example, is no higher than in those treated surgically[15].

One of the things that confuses — and sometimes angers — the public is when 'experts disagree'. In any sphere a journalist who tries hard enough can always find an expert who disagrees with official reports, no matter how independent and unanimous they are.

More importantly, there may be two equally reputable experts who agree completely about just how small a particular risk is, yet talk to journalists as if they strongly disagree. One of them may feel that the situation should be described as reasonably safe, another as not safe. One may prefer 'serious', another 'not serious'. There is no great mystery about this. Neither is being inaccurate. But each of them, when deciding on the words that seem appropriate, is making all kinds of value judgements. One of them hates to see excessive fear. The other would rather see excessive fear than 'complacency'.

There are other reasons why some experts may wish to emphasise risk rather than safety. In every country some may have political or fund-raising reasons for their choice of words. Or perhaps, like the media, they want to feel on the same side as those who are alarmed — rather than be accused of being patronising or unsympathetic. They may also want to do what they can to get financial help for those suffering hardship, even if the real reason for the hardship is not radiation (not directly anyway) but evacuation. Others may be so concerned about the outside possibility that they might one day be proved wrong, that they play safe and avoid saying anything reassuring. And some may feel in some vague way (consciously or unconsciously) that fear of radiation, even if it is excessive, lessens the risk of a nuclear holocaust.

Finally, there is the problem of evacuation and relocation of exposed populations. Quite apart from the fairly remote possibility of another Chernobyl accident, it is only wishful thinking that can stop us now from facing up to a much more serious possibility — the possibility that sooner or later in an unstable world some fanatical group may beg, borrow or steal a nuclear device and use it for blackmail or for revenge. We need to think hard about what to do in areas of dilute radiation well clear of areas of destruction. The problem is to achieve a sensible balance between the distress, hardship and economic consequences of mass evacuation and the probably very small risk for the individual of carrying on as normal. In the former USSR such decisions are now having to be based more on the likely psychological impact than on an objective balance of advantages and disadvantages[10].

It will not be easy, but if the public can be persuaded that the risks of dilute radiation are not nearly as great as they have been led to believe, it might be possible, when considering the size of the area — if any — to be evacuated, to have much less drastic guidelines than would be acceptable in the present climate of excessive fear.

We must not make the old mistake of prescribing for others what we would not want for ourselves. No analogy with radiation risks is entirely satisfactory, but the cancer risks of smoking and the cancer risks of radiation have both been particularly well studied, so we could reasonably ask ourselves this question. How many of us would want to be evicted from our homes (and not be allowed to return) if the risk of staying was probably no more (and perhaps considerably less) than that of smoking a very occasional cigarette — or living with a cigarette smoker?

References

1. Brewin TB. When and how should we teach the basic concepts of radiation beam dosage? *Br J Radiol* 1977; **50**: 430–4

2.   Brewin TB. Radiotherapy and oncology. *BMJ* 1983; **286**: 443–4

3.   Barsky AJ. The paradox of health. *N Engl J Med* 1988; **318**: 414–18

4.   Taylor LS. Some non-scientific influences on radiation protection standards and practice. *Health Phys* 1980; **39**: 851–74

5.   Covello VT. Communicating information about the health risks of radioactive waste: a review of obstacles to public understanding. *Bull N Y Acad Med* 1989; **65**: 467–83

6.   Dunster HJ. The appreciation of radiation risks. *J R Coll Physicians Lond* 1990; **24**: 154–5

7.   Sorensen JA. Perception of Radiation Hazards. *Semin Nucl Med* 1986; **16**: 158–70

8.   Consumers Association. *Radiation, part of Life.* London: Consumers Association, 1965

9.   Watt Committee on Energy. *Five years after Chernobyl: 1986–1991.* London: Watt Committee on Energy, 1991 (Savoy Hill House, WC2)

10. International Atomic Energy Agency. *The International Chernobyl Project. Assessment of radiological consequence and evaluation of protective measures.* Vienna: International Atomic Energy Agency, 1991

11. Neel JV, *et al.* The genetic effect of the atomic bombs. In: Baverstock KF, Stather JW, eds. *Low dose radiation: biological bases of risk assessment.* London: Taylor and Francis, 1989

12. Senturia YD, Peckham CS, Peckham MJ. Children fathered by men treated for testicular cancer. *Lancet* 1985; **ii**: 766-9

13. British Medical Association. *Living with risk,* London: John Wiley & Sons, 1987

14. Berry RJ. The radiologist as guinea pig: radiation hazards to man as demonstrated in early radiologists and their patients. *J R Soc Med* 1986; **79**: 506–9

15. Dobyns BM, Sheline GE, Workman JB, Tompkins EA, McConahey WW, Becker DV. Malignant and benign neoplasms of the thyroid in patients treated for hyperthyroidism. *J Clin Endocrinol Metab* 1974; **38**: 976–98

Empirical: one word, two meanings

Reprinted from
the Journal of the Royal College of Physicians of London,
1994, Vol 28, pages 78–79

The first dictionary definition of the word 'empirical' is 'based or relying on observation and experience rather than on theory', from the Latin *empiricus*. Used in this sense the word is scientifically impeccable, conveying no hint of unreliability. Here are three contemporary examples of this usage.

'Throughout his career he has been an outspoken critic of loose thinking, in particular of claims made without adequate empirical evidence' [1]

'True empiricism discovers things through repeated, critically evaluated, experiences' [2]

'Proof is rarely discussed today in medicine or in any other branch of empirical science—clinical decisions are made on the basis of acceptable evidence, preferably from properly controlled studies' [3]

However, confusion reigns because so many other writers use the word 'empirical' in a disparaging, pejorative sense to imply a lack of scientific rigour. It would be bad enough if such writers dismissed findings simply because they did not square with any known theory of action. But it is not just that. They seem to think that empirical evidence is intrinsically of poor quality — rather in the way that evidence may be spoken of as 'purely anecdotal'.

Yet another shade of meaning — this time implying a lack of diagnostic precision — is suggested in a recent leading article in The Lancet: 'Empirical therapy is safe, effective, and cheap... The likelihood of missing a treatable cancer is very small' [4]

No 'correct' meaning

Language never stands still and it is usually a mistake to be pedantic and talk only of the 'correct' meaning of a word. The English-speaking world has never attempted to legislate on such matters in the way that the French have. But language should help, not hinder, plain speaking and clarity of thought. It should not enshrine ambiguity and perpetuate confusion.

Some urge more empiricism in medicine, others less. Yet far from disagreeing about the way medicine should be going, they are more likely to be in complete agreement. For example, the writer of a historical review, when discussing puerperal fever, described how Semmelweis 'used the principles of clinical empiricism to determine what caused the specific disease'[5]; and in a review of modern psychiatry, a strong plea was made for this specialty to be placed in future on a 'solid, wholly empirical basis'[6]. It is clear that the last thing either of these writers intended was that their readers should think they were using 'empirical' in a derogatory or unscientific sense. Yet in a recent Harveian Oration delivered to the Royal College of Physicians, it was said of the earliest days of medicine: 'the primitive practitioner was the witch doctor...In banishing evil spirits empirical methods were often used'[7]. And when the speaker came to review medical progress in recent centuries he no longer used the word 'empirical', implying that an important element of progress has been to get away from it.

Why do we continue to tolerate, almost without comment, this bizarre situation in current medical writing where the word 'empirical' is used in quite different ways, one approving, one disapproving? What will future generations make of it? They will no doubt be aware that, over time, words may change their meaning but they will surely think it very strange, if not thoroughly confusing, when they see medical writers throughout the twentieth century persistently using the same word to represent almost opposite concepts.

Do dictionaries throw any light on this conflict between different meanings? They do. Surprisingly, one of the secondary meanings given for empirical in the Oxford English Dictionary is 'guilty of quackery'[8]. Lewis drew attention to this paradox more than 25 years ago. 'It is a pity', he wrote, 'that the word "empiric" has had a bad meaning as well as a good one for the past four hundred years: it has been as likely to denote a quack as to be applied to a close and dispassionate observer'[9]. More recently the Oxford Companion to Medicine put it this way: 'Post-Hippocratic empiricists rejected theory and based their system on observation and experiment. Despite the modern ring to this, empiricism later became synonymous with ignorance, unscientific thought and quackery'[10].

Beyond mere semantics?

Does not this remarkable switch in meaning occurring four hundred years ago reveal something rather significant in the history of medicine — something that goes far beyond mere semantics? The explanation must be the tendency — still sometimes seen today — to regard treatment based on theory not just as more respectable in some misguided 'scientific' sense, but actually as more reliable than what one dictionary definition unbelievably refers to as 'mere experience'. In fact, basing practice too much on theory is one of the great errors of medicine[11]. Far too often, treatment based on some theory, without proper comparative testing to show its true worth, has later (sometimes not till much later) been recognised as ineffective.

So should not the surprisingly popular derogatory use of the word 'empirical' be phased out? Not just for the sake of semantic correctness, but to sort out the present confusion in which some writers use the word in one way, some in another. *'Based on experience, not on theory'* is a clear and unambigious statement; there is no reason to read into it anything unreliable or unscientific. It is the quality of the experience and the conclusions that can be reliably drawn from it which need special attention.

References

1. Attallah N. *Of a certain age.* London: Quartet Books, 1992. 118.

2. Whorton JC. in *Examining holistic medicine,* Stalker D, Glymour C (eds). Buffalo, New York: Prometheus Books, 1989.

3. Friedlander ER. *Ibid.*

4. Leading article. Negative investigations. *Lancet* 1992; **340**: 213.

5. Benrubi GI. Escape from dogma—the development of clinical empiricism and basic science in American medicine 1830-1910. *J Florida Med Ass* 1989; **76**: 705–11.

6. Polonio P. Body-mind problems from an empirical point of view. *Brit J Psychiat* 1971; **118**: 7–10.

7. Walton JN. *Method in medicine.* London: Royal College of Physicians, 1990.

8. *Oxford English dictionary* (2nd edn). Oxford: Oxford University Press, 1989.

9. Lewis A. Empirical or rational? *Lancet* 1967; ii: 1–9.

10. Walton JN, Beeson PB, Bodley Scott R, Eds. *Oxford companion to medicine.* Oxford: Oxford University, Press, 1986.

11. Todd J. The errors of medicine. *Lancet* 1970; i: 665–70.

SIR —

He was 90 years old. As a young man he had been decorated for courage in battle, but as he got older his great fear was that he might one day develop cancer (how much easier it would be to practise good hospital medicine if all referral letters, not just this one, gave two such helpful pieces of information).

A biopsy specimen of an ulcer on his lip confirmed squamous cell carcinoma. No need for surgery or admission to hospital. After a short course of radiotherapy it would heal, and probably never cause him any further trouble. *"It's not cancer, is it?"*, he asked, his eyes moist with tears. And emphatically, without the slightest hesitation or qualification (which would have been fatal to effective reassurance), I assured him that it was not.

Was this a blatant, but some would say justifiable, lie? On the contrary, was it not the truth? He had what the medical profession calls cancer. He did not have what he meant by cancer. He did not have a shameful, painful, fatal disease that would soon spread. Or anything like it. For him it was more truthful to say that it was not cancer than it would have been to say that it was.

I do not believe that anyone, no matter how good a communicator and no matter how much time spent over it, could have told this man that it was cancer, but curable, without leaving him with a false and untrue impression. Would it not have been somewhat foolish and arrogant to have attempted, at this stage in this man's life, to change his long-held view of what was meant by the word? Speaking to him in his own language (a mark of respect, not of paternalism) he did not have what he had always dreaded. He was not being shielded from the truth. He was being given the truth. Does firm, unhesitating, pragmatic common sense of this kind still have a place in medical practice? Or is it now becoming impossible given the current, rather rigid, unimaginative, time consuming, and sometimes self-defeating attempts to explain everything to everybody?

(Letter to the Editor, *The Lancet* 1994 **343** 1512)

Voluntary euthanasia

Reprinted from
The Lancet,
1986, Vol i, pages 1085–1086

Anyone not aware of all the persuasive arguments in favour of legalising voluntary euthanasia should read two recently published books[1,2]. So should anyone not aware of all the equally persuasive arguments against it; for many of these, too, are set out here, though less prominently. Certainly, no thoughtful reader will ever again jump to conclusions — or easily forget the overriding impression of complexity, paradox, and ambivalence.

Probably most of us, most of the time (whether doctors, nurses, or relatives of a suffering patient) are against 'active' euthanasia. 'Passive' euthanasia, on the other hand — though we might not always want it called that — is something we go along with, perhaps even strongly favour, if it will diminish the risk of pointless suffering or prolongation of dying.

In *The End of Life*[1] James Rachels, professor of philosophy in the University of Alabama (readers of the *New England Journal of Medicine* may recall the lively correspondence which followed his article on this subject in 1975), argues that it is very illogical of us to make this distinction between active and passive. Well, so it is. Logically there is little or no difference. But our gut instinct tells us that there is. And, like it or not, we are not going to be browbeaten into changing our minds by mere logic; nor even by the remarkable fact that, whereas in the case of human beings passive euthanasia is widely regarded as a civilised and humane compromise, in the case of animals the same thing is considered an inexcusable cruelty (punishable by law in many countries because it means a slow death rather than a quick merciful one).

Voluntary Euthanasia[2], the other book, is something different — an expanded version of a multiauthor text that the Voluntary Euthanasia

Society first published in 1969. There are now 17 contributors — 7 doctors, 3 lawyers, 3 theologists, 2 philosophers, a politician, and a journalist. As in the first edition, the Society has been generous in the amount of space it has given to its critics. For example, a highlight is a 58-page ding-dong battle between Yale Kamisar, a US lawyer giving his objections to voluntary euthanasia legislation (most of them pragmatic and legal, rather than philosophical or religious) and Glanville Williams, a UK lawyer arguing strongly for it. Each writes well and each pours scorn on the various points put forward by the other, until the reader grows dizzy, trying to balance argument and counterargument. As in the 1969 edition, the adjective voluntary is stressed: in other words, defective babies and demented senior citizens do not come into the argument. What the Society wants is for the mentally competent to be free to make a 'rational choice', either when they are ill, or by means of an 'advance declaration'. Two types of 'living will' (as the latter is often called in the USA) are offered in the form of statements that healthy people can sign. One conforms with existing law. All it really boils down to is a request for the sort of determined symptom relief and 'passive euthanasia' that most compassionate doctors and most religious leaders would probably agree with anyway, provided that the situation is sufficiently hopeless and distressing. The other form specifically requests the 'administration of euthanasia' in certain circumstances and is therefore asking for what is still in most countries (though no longer in Holland) a serious criminal offence.

In a historical review, Gillon[2] shows that the human race has always been hopelessly ambivalent about these things. Some primitive peoples have been in favour of both suicide and euthanasia, some bitterly against. To some, each has been regarded as a noble act, to others a despicable crime. Throughout history philosophers and religious leaders have been equally inconsistent. Interestingly enough, Gillon himself, in a footnote explaining that his chapter was written in 1969, emphasises that his approach would be very different were he to write on the subject today. He is now not sure in which way, if any, he would wish the law to be changed. Another medical contributor (David H. Clark, a psychiatrist) writes in the same vein: "As the years have gone by", he says, "I have seen the complexities and difficulties of this subject and realise why many compassionate physicians oppose legislation, even though they are not constrained by any doctrine or faith".

Some of those urging a change in the law are very persuasive. But others seem to be a little out of touch with the majority of their fellow-citizens. "He who regards his own extinction as a personal catastrophe", declares one, "has, I believe, a perverted sense of values". Writes another, "How different it would be if *a person could talk over the future with family, friends and relatives, make arrangements, say farewells, take stock of his life, and know that his decision about where and when to end his life was a matter that could be the subject of constructive and sympathetic conference . . .".* Which sounds fine and might work beautifully on some planets, but how often on ours? How many patients really want this? How many families could stand it? The mental anguish for friends and relatives — often, we may be sure, upset, ambivalent, guiltridden, and disagreeing with each other — could be horrific.

Those campaigning for legalised voluntary euthanasia claim that public support for it has risen sharply in both the UK and the USA in recent years — from 35–50% to 60–70%. But — whatever people may say in opinion polls when they are not under stress — how many relatives of a suffering patient actually find themselves wishing that the law allowed formal 'active' euthanasia? They may well feel that in some ways death would be a merciful release. Much depends on the quality of care. But even when this is poor and the person they love (father, mother, husband, wife, or child) has been heard to say that he or she wants to die, how many wish that the law allowed for independent legal and medical referees to come and question the patient before presenting a form for signature?

Those who urge the legalising of voluntary euthanasia nearly convince me, but not quite. Not quite, because of a combination of factors. Apart from painful and insensitive formalities (usually felt necessary to ensure that the person concerned really does want life to be extinguished), the 'slippery slope' argument still concerns many of us and a skilful 10-page analysis of this aspect by Rachels failed to reassure me. Then there is the frequent lack of certainty about the prognosis, as regards both quantity and quality of life (though perhaps we should not make too much of this in view of the way in which we often decide that, on balance, it would be wiser and kinder not to go on trying to cure a patient). What about the subtle pressures that might be imposed on old people to remove themselves from the scene for the sake of others? It is surely unrealistic to suggest, as Mary Rose Barrington, a lawyer, does[2] that, *"voluntary euthanasia . . . is concerned exclusively with cases where a patient is a burden to himself . . . whether or not he is a burden to others plays no part whatever"* (my emphasis).

Another point. In advanced cancer certainly (and probably in all 'hopeless' situations, though my own experience is mainly with cancer), friendly professional care, with a positive attitude and an interest in every symptom, can reduce suffering and raise morale to an astonishing degree. Might not legalisation of euthanasia cause some doctors to try less hard?

As for the 'advance declaration' or 'living will', some of its defects and dangers seem to be insufficiently recognised. For example, to take incurable cancer again, why do so many healthy people say they would end their life "*rather than suffer in this way*", yet so very few patients ever make the slightest attempt to take an overdose, even when (as is often the case when the patient is at home) a large stock of morphine tablets and other strong drugs is readily available to them?

Finally, there are the very real fears that many people (especially old people) have about what goes on behind hospital walls — fears sometimes dating from childhood. Might these not increase sharply if regular and officially approved euthanasia was known to take place there — the white-coated doctor with a lethal injection in his hand? And how would other patients in the hospital at the time feel about it? It would surely be best if doctors and hospitals had nothing to do with it.

But what is the alternative? A trip to a specially fitted room at the back of the Town Hall, with newsmen kept at a discreet distance? No need for anything so distasteful as employing an executioner: kindly officials (after a final check to make sure that the papers are in order and each signature is in the correct place) could lift the patient gently into a comfortably padded electric chair; then even the frailest old lady could emphasise the purely voluntary nature of the act by doing it herself — just a touch on the button and that would be that. To some (presumably), what a triumph for autonomy (whose life is it anyway?). But to most of us, how repugnant. To the humane doctor (or to anyone else willing to face realities and not just indulge in philosophical debate) the practicalities of any legislation — the actual mechanics of it — are just as important as the principles involved. Perhaps the way that most good doctors already act is more in tune with the ambivalent mood of society than are the views of some of their critics. Rachels says that there are on record in the USA only 2 cases of doctors ever being accused in court of mercy killing and in both cases they were acquitted — not for lack of evidence, but because the juries refused to convict. Both in the UK and the USA the law says one thing and juries, whenever they feel like it, say another. It is all very untidy and illogical. But might not a change in the law do more harm than good?

References

1. The end of life. By James Rachels, University of Alabama, Birmingham, USA. Oxford: Oxford University Press, 1986.

2. Voluntary euthanasia. Edited by A. B. Downing and Barbara Smoker. London: Peter Owen, 1986.

Sanctity of life

Reprinted from
the Medico-Legal Journal,
1991, Vol 59, pages 36–40

The problem of when to cling to the principle of sanctity of life — and when to forget it — is not new. It has been highlighted by the dilemmas presented by cardiopulmonary resuscitation. The concept of not striving (officiously or otherwise) to preserve life has always been present in at least four main situations, which I shall call here — with brutal brevity — Defective, Disabled, Demented or Dying.

Under the heading Defective I have in mind those new born infants so abnormal that the immediate instinctive feeling of many nurses, doctors and relatives has always been that it is better that they should not survive. By disabled I mean those adults who feel that their life is now so restricted and distressing (due, perhaps, to severe stroke or multiple sclerosis) that they do not want anything done to prolong it. By demented I mean those patients — often very elderly — who no longer recognise members of their own family, who have lost control of their bodily functions, and whose lives seem to be devoid of all pleasure and meaning, so that we have to ask whether, for example, giving them antibiotics for chest infection — or surgery for acute obstruction — is what we would want for ourselves if we were in their position. Are we in danger of just using these people as tokens or symbols — symbols of the sanctity of life?

But having spent most of my professional life treating cancer patients (many of them cured, but many others dying of their disease) it is the fourth category — that of the dying — that I know best and will be mainly considering here.

Different responses

Whenever one of these situations is debated, there seem to me to be three

---

117

main kinds of response — that of the Fundamentalist, that of the Gut Reactionist, and that of the Pragmatist.

Fundamentalists tend to put one principle (usually sanctity of life) far ahead of all others. For them the argument that exceptions should sometimes be made is either unacceptable or deeply worrying. They also fear the slippery slope of a decline in moral standards; but forget that, for some of us at least, moral standards apply just as much to human suffering as to sanctity of life, so that talk of the slippery slope does little or nothing to solve the dilemma when the two conflict.

Gut Reactionists are not much interested in abstract principles; they have no wish to analyse or debate; or even to look too closely into all the details of a situation. Like the fundamentalists, they are not easily swayed by argument or logic. They just have instinctive feelings, which they hold strongly. But they often disagree with each other. What one feels is absolutely right, another finds repellent. Consider, for example, attitudes to human life and human suffering compared with attitudes to animal life and animal suffering. Our feelings of love and compassion may be almost identical. Yet when incurable animals suffer, active euthanasia is judged to be humane and passive euthanasia to be cruel (because it means a slow death rather than a quick merciful one) — while when men or women suffer, the law takes exactly the opposite view as to which is right and which is wrong; which is a criminal offence and which is not.

To what extent is this paradox due to an unconscious, but deep seated instinct to preserve our superior status and never do to humans what we do to animals? I believe that this is a powerful factor in the 'gut reaction' feeling of many people without much religious belief. Consider the outcry not long ago when it was revealed that a veterinary surgeon had assisted at a surgical operation on a human being. Imagine the public reaction if certain antibiotics or other drugs were labelled (as might be perfectly correct) *'suitable for either humans or animals'*. My guess is that that this is one of the reasons why cold, calculated legalised mercy killing would be deeply upsetting to many patients and families — whether or not they had any religious or ethical scruples.

Yet there are other gut reactionists who hold, equally strongly, the opposing view. When all efforts to relieve distressing symptoms fail (as must occasionally happen, even in the best hands) it makes no sense to them that humans should be expected to suffer more than animals.

Pragmatists are not too keen on rules or guide lines. They try to suppress their own gut reactions, but in any dilemma they carefully consider those of others involved. They aim to think only in terms of consequences — both short term and long term — for all concerned. They are not afraid to compromise. They combine compassion with what we used to call wisdom; sound judgment; or just common sense. Concepts impossible to define, but very real to most people.

How certain is it that the outlook is hopeless? How bad is the patient's suffering? What more can be done? How long has this suffering been going on? How much more can she stand? How mentally and physically weak and exhausted is she? How frightened? How disorientated? What seemed to be his view before he was ill? Does this still hold good? Many of these 10 questions may be impossible to answer with any certainty. But all are part of the equation if a wise decision is to be made. And all call for professional medical assessment, based on sensitivity, experience and expertise. A training in philosophy, or ethics, or the law is of little help.

And for the pragmatic physician it doesn't end there. Even more difficult points may have to be considered, often hard to discuss openly and easily misrepresented. The feelings and personalities of the family and others involved. The interests of other suffering patients. Apparent inconsistencies and contradictions are inevitable.

Ambivalence

These responses are not necessarily those of three different people. Few of us are guided all the time by just one of them. The person who is sure of their ground in a public debate may have doubts in a real situation. Even the most committed fundamentalists or gut reactionists — whether doctors, nurses, friends or relatives — can occasionally (and in some cases quite often) be convinced by special circumstances. They may be distressed by what pragmatists advise. Very occasionally they may go to the extent of open disagreement or protest. But more often — when they see that the dilemma is very real and that it is not kind, or not possible, to expect a decision from the patient — they prefer not to rock the boat. Better, they feel, just to be glad that it is not they who have to make a decision.

Unfortunately, at the end of life, no matter what phrases we use (*'helping the patient to die peacefully'*, *'easing the passing'*, *'helping the dying person on his way*' and so on) our words can very easily be made to sound insincere — even sinister — and the popular press often play on this.

The phrase 'passive euthanasia' also causes confusion. It may well have a place in philosophical argument[1], but in the real world of human ambivalence (with many tender emotions and complex feelings of love and guilt) most health staff and relatives prefer to think of what is done as being either appropriate — what they would want done if the patient was someone they love in their own family — or inappropriate.

Difficult decisions

Not just at the end of life, but in many other situations, doctors have to make all kinds of decisions concerning starting, stopping, or modifying treatment. For example, with cancer — even sometimes in quite early stages — we may feel that it is wiser not to attempt to eradicate all the disease, the reason being the poor chance of success and our concern for quality of life. We don't want 'the treatment to be worse than the disease'. There can never be total certainty that a situation is hopeless or that a new treatment will not be discovered. And there will always remain the possibility that a patient who appears to want to die would later have changed their mind. There are no certainties, only probabilities.

And near the end of a long illness (though the media may later talk of a patient having *'finally lost his battle against cancer'*) the reality may be very different. All who love and respect him may have been hoping for some time that the end will come as soon as possible. Some patients and their families have suffered so much. They are so weary of it all . The thought of yet another brief postponement of death is abhorrent. Everyone feels that enough is enough. We may decide, for example, not to give antibiotics when pneumonia *'comes as a friend'*; and not to start tube feeding or intravenous drips when these would be likely just to add to the patient's discomfort.

However, the doctors and nurses looking after such a patient voice this view — if at all — privately and reverently. They don't spell it out. They don't say, *"are we all agreed? — the sooner he dies the better"*. And they may well be upset if others talk like this. No matter how right it may be, it can sound wrong — or at least insensitive. Relatives, too, though they may be relieved to know that all attempts to prolong life have been abandoned, will frequently not want this to be said too bluntly.

Taking risks with life

If a young man has pain due to acute appendicitis, safety is probably more important than sleep. If an old man has pain due to advanced cancer, sleep is probably more important than safety. Often it is not a question of knowingly shortening life in the interest of relieving pain or other symptoms. It is more a matter of accepting a risk. In routine major surgery, if we did not accept a small risk (sometimes a high risk) of causing death, we could not carry on; and patients would die, not from surgery, but from lack of it. The same sort of thinking applies to taking risks when the aim is relief of suffering. Aim and circumstances justify the risk. This is not euthanasia. And nearly all, if not all, religions, laws and moral guidelines — world wide — approve. Nobody says that suffering is always preferable to risking life.

In the case of morphine, we now know that when the dose is correctly escalated until relief is obtained, the risk to the patient who needs it — even from very big doses is small. The views given by expert medical witnesses called by the prosecution at the trial of Dr Bodkin Adams in 1957[2] were those of most doctors at that time, but we now know them to have been wrong. The defence, though successful (contrary to public expectations) would be in an infinitely stronger position today.

Nevertheless, it is common for relatives or nurses to think that life has been deliberately shortened or death accelerated when, in fact, this is not so. Symptom relief is the aim. And there is seldom any way of knowing whether or not life was, in fact, shortened. When a patient could die at any time, the junior nurse who gives a large dose of morphine may worry if death occurs soon afterwards. And if the doctor herself decides to give what may be the last injection — to spare the nurse such feelings — this may sometimes reinforce the probably wrong assumption that active euthanasia is being carried out.

Who decides?

Ideally, the patient's view is what counts. But every experienced doctor and nurse knows that in many real life situations it is either impossible, or unrealistic, or just unthinkable to try to obtain this. The recent 'Living Will' campaign (mainly in the USA, but spreading now to the UK and other countries) can sometimes give some guidance to a person's attitude to resuscitation or attempts to prolong their life, should their outlook (either for survival or for severe disability) ever become very bad. But inevitably the sort of situations that may arise are oversimplified. Moreover new laws can have the opposite effect to that intended — those who have not made such a declaration being at increased risk of being kept alive in a way that they would probably not have wished.[3]

When it comes to difficult decisions, those with a knowledge of law, ethics, philosophy, or theology may have a part to play, but it is those with the greatest experience of the likely consequences for all concerned (short term and long term) who are needed more than anyone else. They are the ones who have seen the greatest amount of suffering, who have learned from their mistakes, who have seen that things don't always work out as expected.

The lonely 'captain of the ship' decision by a single individual, though it sometimes has much to recommend it (protecting others from the stress of indecision and possible later guilt) is currently frowned upon — at least when debates are held to discuss general principles. Fortunately, in an actual situation, when the problems of what should be done — or not done — are discussed informally by a doctor and senior nurse together (or by a small 'jury' of those most involved) different opinions are rare. Compassion and common sense prevail. Everyone feels the same way. Conflicting moral principles fade into the background.

Mercy killing

As to active euthanasia, of the type considered merciful and humane in the case of suffering animals, there are many persuasive arguments (some philosophical, some pragmatic) both for and against changing the law[4], but the present balance of likely harm and benefit favours leaving it as it is. The caring pragmatic doctor who tries to follow Lister's Rule (*"there is only one rule of good medical practice — put yourself in the patient's place"*) — and who dislikes, or fears, the thought of doing anything without the full and unequivocal sanction of the law — may sometimes feel that the law should be changed. But there are many examples of doctors abandoning this view as they gain more experience and see the practical complexities and snags more clearly[5]. Public opinion, whatever people say in opinion polls when they are well, is deeply ambivalent.

Nobody seems to be able to frame new laws that don't run straight into all kinds of practical or emotional dangers and difficulties[5]. A change in the law might protect doctors and help a few patients. But the overall result might be an increase rather than a decrease in the total amount of distress and unhappiness, physical or mental, for patients and their families.

Recently, a sensitive article by twelve American physicians[6] says that all but two of them believe that it is not immoral for a physician to assist in the rational suicide of a terminally ill patient; but in spite of feeling this they don't urge that the law should be changed.

Conclusion

All of us — professional or lay — want to respect the sanctity of life, but at the same time hate to see pointless suffering. When these two come into conflict — and one of them has to give way — each of us may at first seem to draw the line at a different point. But in an actual situation those most involved usually agree.

The practical and emotional difficulties of any new legislation are so great that it is probably best to accept the inherent ambivalence in the present situation. There are too many conflicting ethical principles regarding what is done and not done (and too many subtle variations in each situation) for routine efforts by committees, or courts, or ethical experts, to disentangle them. Doctors, nurses and other health workers are the best people to face these problems, however imperfectly. It is part of their job. They have the greatest first hand, on the spot, experience. They are also best placed to assess (from real life situations rather than from opinion polls) any changes there may be in public attitudes. But they must on occasion be prepared, like everyone else, to answer to the courts.

References

1. Rachel J. *The End of Life*. Oxford: Oxford University Press, 1986.

2. Devlin P. *Easing the Passing: the trial of Dr John Bodkin Adams*. London: Bodley Head, 1985.

3. Heintz LL. Legislative Hazard: keeping alive against their wills. *Journal of Medical Ethics* 1988; **14**: 82–86.

4. Voluntary Euthanasia. Ed. Downing AB and Smoker B. London: Peter Owen, 1986.

5. Brewin TB. Voluntary Euthanasia. *Lancet* 1986; **1**: 1085–86.

6. Wanzer SH *et al*. The Physician's Responsibility toward Hopelessly ill patients. *New England Journal of Medicine* 1989; *320*: 844–849.

How much ethics is needed to make a good doctor?

Reprinted from
The Lancet,
1993, Vol 341, pages 161–163

The most caring doctor may be totally ignorant of academic ethics. And this should come as no surprise. Has anyone ever said about a friend or neighbour that the reason he is so thoughtful and kind is that he has studied ethics?

By a good doctor I mean one who is regarded as such by patients and by their relatives, by nurses and paramedical staff, and by other doctors. And I am thinking particularly of what the average doctor means when saying of two specialist colleagues that A is the better expert, but B is the better doctor. I suggest that this comment refers to qualities coming under the broad headings of motivation, judgment, and rapport.

Motivation, judgment, and rapport

Motivation of the right kind includes being caring and attentive and following Lister's rule of good medical practice: put yourself in the patient's place. Sound judgment includes assessment, advice, and decisions, especially in the face of doubts or contradictory findings — always tempered with a regard for other patients, present and future. A good rapport with patients includes all aspects of communication, but especially a blend of adequate information, encouragement, and a sensitive regard for changing moods and emotional needs.

To what extent can the teaching of ethics produce — or encourage — these qualities? It depends how we define it. In one sense ethics is such an integral part of medicine that we can never have too much of it. In this sense it should be taught constantly by those men and women in society who practise (or have practised) medicine — and who therefore have the greatest experience of making difficult medical decisions and learning from their mistakes. This includes not only good doctors — as just defined — but also other health workers with experience of major clinical decision-making.

These men and women should not only influence students by the example they set; they should also have a talent for teaching and for recounting instructive anecdotes, especially about occasions when things did not turn out as expected, or when paradox and ambivalence added to the difficulty of making a decision. When the results of one treatment policy are being compared with another, anecdotal evidence can easily lead to false conclusions; but good anecdotal teaching about ethical dilemmas can be of great value.

Academic ethics

Then there is what might be called academic ethics, a subject with the approach and terminology of non-medical ethics, usually taught by those who have studied ethics but not practised medicine. There is a growing belief that medical schools ought to spend more time on it. But will this produce better doctors? Certainly, it is valuable to have one or two lectures and discussions to show how different societies in human history have come to different compromises over such eternal dilemmas as those involving the sanctity of life. But, to take the first of my three points, will academic ethics improve motivation? The notion strikes me as naive. Motivation depends on many things, including — as in many other occupations — the desire to have a good reputation and the satisfaction of receiving heartfelt thanks from a fellow human being who sought your help (marvellous when you really deserve it, not so good when you don't).

What about the second quality — sound judgment? It is not easy to see how studying academic ethics can be of much help. Merely treating the disease, for example, without fully considering the patient, is bad medicine because fewer patients are helped — and even these are not as much helped as they could have been. There does not seem to be any great need to call this ancient (but all too common) error less ethical, or less humane, or less in tune with some particular philosophy. It just means that less is achieved; and that there is a greater risk of doing more harm than good.

Take another example. When forming an opinion as to what risks are justifiable — or when trying to decide whether or not to advise some drastic measure when the chance of cure is slim — what help is academic ethics? What possible help, for example, is it to have learned at medical school the word "non-malefiscence" — a piece of ethical jargon that has always seemed to me as ugly as it is useless? Is the answer to put complex problems to patients and insist that it is they who must decide? If so, how much detail do we give? To what extent do we simplify the problem for them? The wishes of patients are sovereign and always have been. There is nothing new in that concept. But to what extent do we influence their decisions? There are no rules. No easy answers.

Here we come to the third and final quality — the all important matter of rapport with the patient. Whatever the rhetoric, an essential element of trust is trust in the doctor not to be heartless and clumsy when discussing hopes, fears, and options. In other words, not to be indiscriminate with "the truth" (the quotes are very necessary) and not to put abstract principles before the needs of individuals. To ethical fundamentalists the patient has a right to all the evidence (hard or soft), all the suspicions, all the doubts, all the gloom. But, even today, when for many ill patients there is more need than ever before to try and explain as much as possible of the reasoning behind each piece of advice, those who overdo it can create havoc — until they learn tact and sensitivity.

Let us be honest: hardly anyone — relative, partner, nurse, or doctor — sticks rigidly to total truth-telling. There is often something held back, just as there is in ordinary life. Those who make a point of telling their neighbours everything they "have a right to know" about what is going on around them will not usually be congratulated on their impeccable ethics.

Caring pragmatism

It is caring sensitive pragmatism that makes a good doctor. What is needed in medical schools is thorough discussion of the pros and cons of difficult dilemmas. The more the better. The effects of different decisions on patients and on the duration and quality of their lives. Short-term effects, long-term effects, good effects, bad effects, unexpected effects. The more the better. But the constant recycling of high-sounding ethical principles is of little help — mainly because as rules or guidelines they tend either to contradict each other or to be mere platitudes. Once this is accepted, the idea that philosophers and ethical experts should teach doctors how to make wise decisions begins to crumble. And with it the notion[1] that doctors are unfit to teach it since they are not trained in these subjects.

Just as political activists often abandon their early rhetoric in favour of pragmatism, so — when exposed to more and more real life medical situations — may philosophers and advisers on ethics. For example, Schafer, a philosopher, discards philosophy and tries pragmatism when he writes that "ignorance has a way of generating unwarranted anxieties and fears";[2] and Kennedy, a lawyer, is now less likely to claim that "medicine is, at bottom, a political enterprise" or that "these new codes" (on the care of the terminally ill) "are badly flawed in that they have been drawn up by doctors, so perpetuating the notion that what is involved is a matter of technical expertise".[1] Perhaps such writers would have made good doctors, but they chose another career, and in general, when it comes to pragmatism, it does not seem sensible, in any walk of life, to give high priority to the views of the inexperienced.

In love with words

On occasions, many of us feel the need to follow some noble principle, like soldiers following a flag, rather than be seen doing anything so mundane as compromising afresh in each difficult situation. And many ethicists, when ultimately facing up to the supremacy of pragmatism, may cling to the wreckage of their original principles by talking of, say, the compassionate withholding of information not as pragmatism but as a kind of respect for autonomy. But such semantic somersaults, designed to dress up pragmatism in the clothes of ethical principles, strike me as dishonest and unhelpful.

Sometimes it seems that the appeal of academic ethics is connected with the love of long words, ritual phrases, and classifications for their own sake. For some people such things seem to give comfort and emotional support. There is also perhaps an element of belief that new words represent progress. "When the mind is at sea" wrote Goethe (according to Arthur Koestler), "a new word is like a raft".

But there are disadvantages. One is that academic ethics may make young doctors and nurses feel guilty when, for example, instinct, common sense, and compassion all tell them not to go too far with truth-telling or respect for the sanctity of life. Abstract ethical principles that are too firm may also inhibit the careful weighing of all pros and cons, so necessary before coming to a wise pragmatic decision. Many ethicists will protest that this is not what they intend, but is there not a danger of ethical rules leading to mental laziness — with insufficient thought being given to difficult decisions?

A third danger is that teaching of this kind will discourage the firm "captain of the ship" decisions that many frightened and confused patients (including many doctors when they are ill) and hospital staff still expect from the leader of a team in certain situations, however unfashionable and however unattractive to some ethicists. This is not just a medical matter. Whatever the nature of the crisis, help comes from those who have the gift of good judgment, firm leadership, and common sense.

Conclusion

Patients want efficiency, kindness, understanding, and gentleness; and if they have to go through a major ordeal they want to feel that this is only what the doctors involved would want for themselves or their own families. This is what counts.

Let us work hard at the aim of wise advice and sound decisions in particular circumstances — in other words, good medicine, uncluttered by the jargon, slogans, and abstractions of academic ethics. And, in our anxiety not to be arrogant, let us not lose our self-confidence and self-esteem. If we hand over the teaching of medical ethics to outsiders, as some seem to think we should, we send the wrong message to society. For we hand over the core, the kernel, the very heart of good medicine.

References

1. Kennedy I. Unmasking medicine. London: George Allen & Unwin, 1981.

2. Schafer A. Sunday Times, Dec 10, 1989.

Logic and magic in mainstream and fringe medicine

Reprinted from
the Journal of the Royal Society of Medicine,
1993, Vol 86, pages 721–723

Introduction

Qualified medical practitioners follow no fixed belief or system and are free to try any remedy, so mainstream is a better label than orthodox. And fringe is a crisp one syllable title, covering alternative, unconventional, complementary, natural and holistic, and is a name that its admirers were once happy to use[1]. So let's retain it.

There must be many reasons for the current boom in fringe medicine. One is clearly the desire for more attention, more time, more sympathetic understanding, more hope. Another is probably the increasing wish of many patients to be given causes and explanations, even where none is really known and where what is offered is pure speculation.

A third obvious reason, especially in serious illness, is a desperate desire to try something different — anything — often accompanied these days with a longing to feel 'in control', rather than just accepting what has happened and hoping for the best (this latter attitude to misfortune now being rather despised, though it used to be admired).

Finally, I suggest that fringe medicine appeals to that side of our nature that dislikes logic and prefers magic — a basic instinct that may be seeking other outlets following a decline in religious observance.

Logic or magic?

By logic I just mean logical reasoning. Semantic confusion has been caused

---

by labelling as 'rational' or (logical) only those remedies whose mechanism we understand — or think we do — regardless of evidence of effectiveness. But which is more rational? To follow theory or results? We need a word other than 'rational' for treatments that we merely think *ought* to work — according to laboratory experiment or armchair reasoning. Evidence for effectiveness and evidence to support the relevance of some suggested explanatory theory are two different things. They should be kept separate.

Logic looks at all available evidence and considers all possibilities; not just those based on personal conviction, authority or wishful thinking. From the logical side of our nature also comes the urge to question all things, search for clues, sift evidence, get at the truth and tackle challenges, whether intellectual or practical. None of this is much to the liking of fringe medicine — which, consequently, unlike mainstream medicine, makes little or no progress and solves no basic problems. Plenty of grateful patients, yes — but not enough insight or honesty to see the most likely reason for this. Very little convincing testing of remedies; very little self criticism, or learning from mistakes; and too many sweeping all embracing theories, usually contradicting each other and based on belief without adequate supporting evidence.

By magic I am thinking partly of good magic, partly of bad. An example of the first is the way in which some doctors, nurses and fringe practitioners can quickly restore morale, giving immediate hope and peace of mind to those in distress. If that's not magic, it sometimes seems like it. There may well be unknown factors here.

As for bad magic I am thinking mainly of anti-rational attitudes — harmless when confined to astrology or palmistry, but now disturbingly on the increase in the health field. For example, the perverse idea that human life was healthier when it was more natural and less civilized — ignoring the fact that millions of us now enjoy a safer life, a better quality life, and a longer life than did those who came before us. Or the equally strange belief that a healthy mind protects us, not just from some ills, but from all (does this apply to other primates, too?). Or the idea that until medicine cures everything (not merely far more things than ever before) it has failed.

Along with this come all kinds of bizarre theories, diets and rituals, sometimes mixed with pseudo-scientific jargon, sometimes with a smattering of the occult and paranormal. Mystery — instead of being a challenge to puzzle over (or just to marvel at) — is answered by myth. All this is popular with one side of our nature. Lack of good evidence adds to the magic. Don't forget that a certain amount of madness and magic are in our blood. Quite recently in our history (since Shakespeare wrote his plays) hundreds of women were officially designated by both church and state as witches — and burnt[2].

Lack of logic in mainstream medicine

However, let's also look at mainstream medicine. When it comes to logic, how well do we score? For inconspicuous logic and a longing for magic there is perhaps not a lot to choose between the typical claims of so much fringe medicine ('homeopathy can be successful in all diseases'[3]) and the remarkable official aim of the World Health Organization ('Health for all by the year 2000'[4]). And do we, too, not still indulge sometimes in wasteful mumbo jumbo and magic? What about all those almost needless or low priority scans and tests, which impress the patient and symbolize the wonders of modern technology, but which we know are very unlikely to alter outcome[5]? Do such tests not sometimes soak up much badly needed money and resources?

As for logic, perhaps these days mainstream medicine is two parts logic and one part magic, whereas not so long ago it was the other way round. Examples of lack of simple logic are still common. For example, in my own field — cancer — there are still some who think that if earlier diagnosis is followed by longer survival (longer from the date of diagnosis) this must mean that treatment is prolonging life. Or that if one kind of cancer shows 60% five year survival after treatment and another kind only 15% this shows that the first treatment is doing more good than the second. In both cases it may be so, but we need more evidence. Evidence of the kind just given is by itself worthless, containing not even a probability that what is claimed is true.

Another example of simple logic that we cannot duck, however unpalatable, is that no matter how good the evidence that treatment A gets a better result than treatment B, one possible reason for this is that treatment A is useless and that treatment B is doing harm. To sort this out, further evidence is needed. Similarly, you don't need any training in statistical analysis to appreciate that new and more accurate methods of finding out how far a cancer has spread (which will put many patients into a more advanced stage) will appear to improve the results in each stage, even if nobody is any better off.

Again, whether we are looking at mainstream or fringe medicine, honest thinking is all we need to face up to the fact that if an assortment of widely different treatments (or the same drug at widely different doses, or surgery that varies greatly in its scope and thoroughness) all give broadly the same result, then the most likely possibility — or at least one that must be taken seriously — is that all are ineffective. Logic can be painful when it collides with wishful thinking, but is vital if we are to get our priorities right.

Perhaps the most interesting — and humbling — thing about these five examples is that to appreciate their validity requires no scientific or statistical training whatever. Nor do any of them depend on any advances made in the last 100 years. All could have been appreciated by anyone thinking clearly 200 years ago or more.

Comparing results

How are we to assess outcome? The public, the media and even some professionals seem to have little idea of how difficult it can be to know whether or not a treatment is effective — and, if so, how effective. The history of medicine shows that it is quite possible for a remedy that is actually doing harm — never mind not doing any good — to be thought of (by both doctors and patients) as effective. One example is blood letting, a popular treatment for hundreds of years — and it was popular for far more conditions than those few (high blood pressure and so on) for which it could possibly have been of real benefit. Another is traditional remedies applied to cuts and abrasions, probably infecting them and delayed healing — but the pus that appeared was thought to have been 'successfully brought to the surface'.

Quite apart from our old friend the placebo effect[6], three factors stand out. First, many disorders are self limiting. Second, in many chronic conditions spontaneous remissions are common — the last remedy to be used getting the credit. Third, unwarranted assumptions are common, such as the belief that without the treatment symptoms would have persisted or got worse (or that death would have occurred) when, in fact, the usual thing — the normal thing — in most diseases (including cancer) is for a few patients to do, not just better than expected, but far better than expected. In medicine, unexplained miracles are as normal as unaccountable disappointments.

An important factor here is that most of us, whether practitioners or patients, want to believe that it was the remedy that did the trick. This is partly to feel in control, but also — in the case of fringe medicine — to please the side of our nature that craves for magic. Response to a fringe remedy is exciting. Response to a mainstream remedy is merely satisfactory. Spontaneous recovery, on the other hand, is frankly boring. Nothing to be enthusiastic about, nothing to recommend to friends. For this reason supporters of natural healing usually take good care to add some remedy or other to the work of nature. They don't want nature to get all the credit.

To get at the truth we nearly always need to make a valid comparison of some kind, both groups being alike apart from how they are treated[7]. Whatever the statistical complexities where small differences are concerned — and whatever the practical and emotional problems — you would think that this basic principle of reliable comparison would have been obvious to thoughtful men and women for centuries. Yet until quite recently hardly anybody saw the need for it — further testimony to the faltering, inconstant, reasoning powers of homo 'sapiens'.

Two kinds of comparison

Having decided what to compare (treatment versus no treatment, drastic treatment versus gentle, new drug versus placebo, one policy versus another policy, and so on) we can then either — in the style of research — look at just one aspect; or — in a very practical way — we can compare all the advantages and disadvantages of two policies[8,9]. Ideally, we should do this not just with every new treatment, whether mainstream or fringe, but with every new technique or investigation.

To compare from the start may well rob many doctors of the chance to publish 'encouraging' preliminary results[9-11]. To the public, however, testing new remedies in this way probably makes far more sense than comparing established ones. Inexperience with a new remedy does not affect the need to compare. Dosage and so on can be adjusted later. It is illogical to suggest that to randomise a pilot trial is unethical. Those who get the new treatment at this stage may later be either glad or sorry. Exactly the same applies to those who don't get it.

The day will probably come — provided we don't slip back into a new dark age — when randomised pilot trials will be standard practice and it will amaze historians that we failed to do them. Anything less will be considered by the public, as well as by the profession, to be both irrational and unethical. This will protect thousands of patients from having treatments for many years that are later recognised to have been second best or needlessly drastic.

Fringe practitioners and others sometimes claim that for them such comparisons are not valid because of variations in treatment to suit the individual. But this statement, though frequently made, does not hold water. No matter how complex and variable what is done (or how often it is modified for each person, or what criteria of success or failure are chosen) how can all benefit, if truly present, suddenly become invisible as a result of a formal comparison being made?

Indeed, there is no reason why a policy of constantly varying the treatment should not be compared with a more standardised policy, the latter probably having the advantage for the patient of being easier, less time consuming and perhaps safer (because everyone in the treating team is familiar with a standard procedure). Such advantages may or may not be outweighed by disadvantages. We need to find out.

Alternatively, whether in mainstream or fringe medicine, one particular aspect of a policy can be looked at to see if it is doing good, or harm, or neither. Some years ago some of us unsuccessfully suggested to those practising fringe medicine at the Bristol Cancer Help Centre that to find out whether or not their very exacting and controversial diet was really helping patients, they could make their own comparison. Some of their patients would take a normal healthy well balanced diet, others the special clinic diet. In every other way they would all get whatever was normally recommended. In particular, all would get the special individualised psychological support and friendly interest for which the clinic is well known. Then the truth would emerge, just as it would in any situation where we wish to test the true value of something complementary or adjuvant.

One of the problems of making formal comparisons, if we are honest, is having to express frank doubts to patients who long for paternalistic certainties. Either we accept this as an overriding objection; or we decide that the ethical balance tips firmly the other way and that we ought to be doing far more to persuade the media and the public of the need for such trials.

Just the disease? or the whole patient?

How important is it to consider the whole patient? Holistic medicine now has an almost mystical sound about it. Perhaps sometimes 'whole' and 'holy' get a bit mixed up, but this question is also largely a matter of simple logic and common sense, with little need for grandiose philosophical, mystical or ethical concepts. People vary. They have different needs and life styles, different problems, different fears, different perceptions. You don't need any fancy jargon to prop up the obvious fact that doctors — like anyone else aiming to help those who seek their help — will have a higher success rate if they consider the whole person, rather than doing the same thing for all those who at first sight have the same problem.

Though fringe medicine would love to think otherwise, holism — if that is what we are now to call it — is a long standing and fundamental tenet of mainstream medicine. True, neither Lister nor Osler, pillars of the medical establishment 100 years ago, ever said that in an ongoing situation it is mandatory to empathise with the personality characteristics of the individual client. However, Lister said that there is only one rule of good medical practice, put yourself in the patient's place. And Osler said that what matters is not what sort of disease the patient has, but what sort of patient has the disease. Which comes to much the same thing.

At the same time we must have sensible priorities. Something is wrong if other patients, perhaps anxious or ill or in pain, are kept waiting while nearly all those being seen — rather than just those where it is important — are flattered (or perhaps irritated) by detailed questions about their personal life. The increase in lengthy low priority chat and documentation of this kind is one of the reasons for accelerating health costs. True, every patient deserves at least a brief word or two about something other than her medical problem — partly to be friendly, partly as a mark of respect, partly as an antidote to fear. However, detailed exploration of social and emotional problems, though sometimes badly needed, can be indulgent and wasteful.

Finally, when a patient is in a situation for which logic and reason have not yet discovered any treatment that alters the course of the disease, can Mainstreamers give as much comfort as Fringe Magicians? Can they compete? Can they make up for the fact that for them it goes against the grain to think up weird and wonderful theories, which at one swoop can provide a cause, an acceptable label, and complex ritual therapy? Can they be equally positive and encouraging, yet remain honest? Can they make similar good use, without overdoing it, of the powerful therapeutic weapon of suggestion? It's not easy, but — given equal concern for the patient and equal charisma — I think they can. Above all, they can if they show sincere, warm, friendly interest — in the patient as a person; in his symptoms; and in his problems, his hopes and his fears. Mainstreamers also have the big advantage of being better trained, especially in the differential diagnosis of symptoms. This can give the patient greater peace of mind through feeling safer in the hands of a fully trained doctor. Whatever happens in fringe medicine, at least in mainstream medicine let's continue to aim for a kind heart combined with a keen intellect - and not sacrifice either to current fads or slogans.

Acknowledgments:

For useful discussions I am indebted to colleagues in *HealthWatch* (previously the *Campaign against Health Fraud*) — John Garrow, Iain Chalmers, Andrew Herxheimer and others — but they will not necessarily agree with my views, nor with how I have expressed them.

References

1. Inglis B. *Fringe Medicine.* London: Faber and Faber, 1964

2. Smout TC. *History of the Scottish People 1560-1830.* London: Collins, 1969

3. Fulder S. *Handbook of Complementary Medicine.* Oxford: Wiley, 1988

4. World Health Organization. *Global Strategy for Health for All by the Year 2,000.* Geneva: WHO, 1981

5. Brewin TB. The cancer patient: too many scans and x-rays. *Lancet* 1981; **ii**: 1098–9

6. Spiro HM. *Doctors, Patients and Placebos.* New Haven and London: Yale University Press, 1986

7. Cochrane AL. Effectiveness and Efficiency. London: Nuffield Provincial Hospitals Trust, 1972

8. Schwartz D, Lellouch J. Explanatory and Pragmatic Attitudes in Therapeutic Trials. *J Chron Dis* 1967; **20**: 637–48

9. Bradford Hill A. The clinical trial. *Practitioner* 1963; **190**: 85–90

10. Chalmers TC. Randomisation of the first patient. *Med Clin N Am* 1975; **69**: 1035–8

11. Spodick DH. Randomize the first patient: scientific, ethical and behavioral bases. *Am J Cardiol* 1983; **51**: 916–17

Fraternizing with fringe medicine

Reprinted from
the British Journal of General Practice,
1994, Vol 44, pages 243–244

Few in mainstream medicine want to give offence by seeming to ridicule patients or healers anxious to believe that fringe medicine — increasingly demanded by the population of many countries[1,2] — can cure illness. So why should we not fraternize with almost anyone who shares our own wish to give hope and comfort, at least whenever nothing better is available?

However, we may be going too far in our anxiety to be less critical than in the past. Perhaps we should not be quite so afraid of being called arrogant or patronizing. The recent report from the British Medical Association[1] tries to be polite about all of the various beliefs and theories that make up fringe medicine, even such things as iridology, which claims to be able to make diagnoses from looking into the eyes, and reflexology, which claims the same from looking at the feet. None of these therapies are endorsed by the British Medical Association, but neither are they criticized. All those on the list are thanked for the information they have sent in, and given a credibility that would have been unthinkable a few years ago.

A firm distinction must surely be made between fully trained, qualified and registered medical practitioners (who are taught differential diagnosis and encouraged to follow, whether in diagnosis or therapy, where the evidence leads) and unqualified healers with fixed beliefs who feel no need to make any such effort.

Do we really want to give the impression that we approve equally of all claims and remedies, no matter how little evidence there is that they are anything more than placebo? Nobody, it seems, dares make the point that in medicine there are a whole range of situations where it is virtually impossible for a remedy, however worthless, not to have many grateful patients. The history of medicine teaches us that there are many circumstances where everyone involved — patients, relatives, doctors, healers — may sincerely believe that there has been a real objective effect on the disease process, when in retrospect this is not true. Those who think that they have been helped may even have been harmed.

Gratitude is an unreliable index. Many patients feel better because of one or more types of placebo: the personality of doctor or healer, the relief at starting a new and exciting remedy, the use of strong verbal suggestion that there will be benefit, tablets of a striking shape or colour, needles, enemas and so on. Another factor that is equally important is that gratitude is often based on the false premise that without the remedy there would have been no improvement. It can also be wrongly assumed that without the treatment relapse would have occurred. Alternatively, those expressing gratitude may be essentially healthy, but may have been persuaded that it is only alternative medicine that keeps them that way.

Those who believe that an unorthodox herbal remedy is more likely to help them than an orthodox herbal remedy (digitalis, for example) must be free to choose. However, nobody can be happy about choice based on misinformation or lack of information.

Too much fraternization can confuse the public and suggest that we have lost confidence in rational thought and pragmatic problem solving. We risk encouraging the damaging and misleading idea of two equally respectable systems, two schools of thought, two valid cultures. If it is felt that weighing evidence is no more than just a current paradigm of Western science and Western medicine, then the alternative must be blind faith and conviction.

Every weakness and fault of fringe medicine can still be found today in mainstream medicine, though not to nearly the same extent as 100 years ago. Mainstream medicine has not been as honest as it should have been about its mistakes, disappointments and failures. Nor has it done enough randomized comparisons of the outcome of different treatment policies[3]. But its record in both cases is considerably better than that of fringe medicine.

Nevertheless, fraternization has its attractions. Mainstream medicine, though it firmly believes in 'curing sometimes, relieving often and comforting always'[4], cannot easily find time to cope with the increasing demand, not just for the essential information and the moral support that have always been such a vital part of the doctor's job, but for far more lengthy comforting and counselling. Perhaps fringe medicine can supply this need. There is also the increasing desire of many patients to be given a firm diagnostic label, even when there is little or no evidence to justify one, and also to be given an explanation of the cause of every illness, however speculative. This may be a new form of paternalism, replacing the benign old style paternalism that consumerism wants to eradicate. Finally, a surprising number of patients seem to be irresistibly drawn to remedies based on ancient beliefs and rituals, pseudoscience, or a mix of both[5]. However misguided, this desire must be acknowledged.

So should we fraternize, but only with selected groups? The problem is where to draw the line. It's not easy, but rather than avoiding the problem completely perhaps we should make some sort of judgement, paying particular attention to such undesirable features as claims to be able to cure almost anything, whatever its cause or nature, with the same treatment; the use of mystical, antirational language; the presence of an all embracing theory with little or no evidence to support it; or belief in the infallibility of the founder of a theory.

We need to be competent and compassionate carers, always sensitive to the real needs, hopes and fears of each and every patient. We also need to be rational and scientific and to concentrate on the many unsolved problems that still exist, following the dramatic improvement in the length and quality of our lives. If we are sometimes reluctant to fraternize with the fringe we must ask our fellow citizens to understand the reasons — reminding them that there is nothing to stop any effective remedy being incorporated into mainstream medicine[6], and urging them not to undermine priorities by slipping back into fallacy and sorcery.

References

1. British Medical Association. *Complementary medicine: new approaches to good practice.* Oxford University Press, 1993.

2. Eisenberg DM, Kessler RC, Norlock FE, *et al.* Unconventional medicine in the United States. *N Engl J Med* 1993; **328**: 246-252.

3. Schwartz D, Lellouch J. Explanatory and pragmatic attitudes in therapeutic trials. *J Chron Dis* 1967; **20**: 637-648.

4. Strauss MB (ed). *Familiar medical quotations.* Boston, MA: Little, Brown and Company, 1968.

5. Coward R. *The whole truth—the myth of alternative health.* London: Faber and Faber, 1989.

6. Ernst E. Complementary medicine. *Lancet* 1993; **341**: 1626.

Consent to randomised treatment

Reprinted from
The Lancet,
1982, Vol **ii**, pages 919–921

Treatment without consent is repugnant — and a criminal offence. But what kind of consent? When is the ordinary kind appropriate — the kind implied in any walk of life when one person seeks the help and advice of another? And when is special consent ('informed' to a greater or lesser degree) required, in spite of its inherent defects and dangers?

Special consent to treatment may be thought of by the patient as a harmless medicolegal ritual or demanded as a vital right. But in certain situations — especially if we describe every treatment hazard (likely, unlikely, or remote) or spell out every unpleasant possibility if treatment is insufficiently aggressive — the very same informed consent that is helpful to one patient may turn out to be a disaster for the peace of mind of another. It is not just a question of creating anxiety, doubts, or lack of confidence — perhaps at a time when morale is already fragile. Serious and lasting misunderstandings can arise; and it is irresponsible for a doctor to say, "it is not my fault if the patient misquotes me or ignores part of what was said". When we decide how much to say and how to say it, compassion and common sense demand that we take full account of the profound emotional impact of certain words and the risk of misunderstanding.

Doctors can hardly be blamed if their experience of these problems — and their desire to put the welfare of their patients before abstract principles or slogans — makes them wary of the idea of compulsory informed consent, especially when demand for it (as in the case of randomised treatment) seems to be at least partly based on misconceptions.

Randomised treatment (for cancer and other conditions) without special consent has always been easy to attack and difficult to defend[1]. It sounds unethical, but to many of us it is often not merely ethically permissible, but ethically preferable. We were convinced of this many years ago, not only by the arguments of Bradford Hill[2] and others[3,4] but also by our own thinking and experience as doctors. Many local ethical committees in the United Kingdom have (until now anyway) agreed. Yet we have apparently made such a bad job of explaining our view that the legal correspondent of *The Lancet* finds the concept "wholly unacceptable" and the reasons given "unconvincing and unsatisfactory"[5].

Part of the trouble, as with communication of diagnosis and prognosis[6], is that our present age — hating secrecy, despising paternalism, and reluctant to take anything on trust — finds it especially difficult to accept that too much information may be as bad as too little. Most people privately recognise this to be true; and when doctor and layman meet in the real world of home or hospital they usually agree. But in the somewhat artificial world of public debate it is often another story and an apparent split may appear.

So should we keep silent — on the grounds that to speak out only invites further misunderstanding and controversy? Or should we decide that, though fighting a rearguard action against the pressure of changing social attitudes, we may as well mount an occasional counter attack and state our views?

Randomised Treatment

Randomisation is thought to mean that the patient is no longer being treated purely for his own good. It is feared he is being "used" — at best for the benefit of future sufferers from his condition, at worst merely to satisfy scientific curiosity — and that, in terms of hazard, benefit, or both, he risks being treated in a way that would not normally be considered appropriate for him. It is thought that some kind of sacrifice is being demanded of him and that he should either be given a full explanation (and the option to volunteer or not as he wishes) or else not randomised.

But when randomised treatment is given according to long-accepted guidelines (all of them obvious to any doctor who cares about his patients) none of these considerations applies, none holds water, all are false; partly because all ignore the "fundamental distinction" emphasised in the Helsinki Declaration[7] and repeated in somewhat similar words by the Medical Research Council[8]. There will always be occasional demarcation difficulties, but a trial where the sole aim of every option is to benefit the patient (all treatments being equally appropriate) is surely quite different from one with other objectives.

The idea that in the practice of medicine there is always — or even usually — a single best treatment for every situation is moonshine. Doctors often have to choose — after discarding what is unsuitable or second best — from several 'best treatments'; and their choice is likely to be influenced by all kinds of factors, including faith, prejudice, habit, and hunch — none of which alter the fact that (within the limits of current knowledge) there is more than one best treatment, "best" always meaning the best balance between hazard and benefit. In a randomised trial, this choice is made by random selection, which helps to avoid the sort of bias which has led in the past to so many false claims. Nobody knows which group of patients will do best. In cancer therapy, especially, even if one group seems at first to be doing a little better, eventual relapse (perhaps merely delayed by the more hazardous treatment) and the onset of late complications of treatment may mean that in the end the other group comes out ahead.

It has always been a central concept of randomised treatment that if, for any reason whatever, one of the policies being compared seems unsuitable, or second best, for a particular patient, then that patient must not be entered into the trial[2]. Provided this is done (and, fortunately, the exclusion of patients *before* randomisation in no way interferes with the vital principle of comparing like with like) the ethics of a randomised trial are merely the ethics of each of the treatments contained in it. The benefit or the hazards of each — and the need for special consent — can all be considered separately on their merits, exactly as they would if no trial was taking place. A method of treatment cannot suddenly become unethical simply because it is included in a randomised trial.

Suppose that two treatments are being compared by randomisation. Perhaps both have been used for many years, one at one centre, one at another (laymen sometimes assume that it is only new treatments whose value is in doubt—would this were true!) and at last both centres have the humility and good sense to accept that there is no reliable evidence (because of different selection) to show whether or not the more hazardous or more expensive option is doing any better than the simpler one. So they agree to do a randomised trial. Or suppose that one treatment is new and experimental (perhaps something like interferon, a much publicised recent possibility in the treatment of cancer) and the other "standard". No amount of preliminary laboratory or animal experiments can accurately predict the hazards of the new drug. As with a new surgical technique, nobody can be sure whether it will turn out to be more effective than existing treatment; about the same; or worse. Randomisation is ethical because it could equally well be that those who receive the new treatment will become increasingly glad that they braved its unknown hazards; or it could turn out that those who do not get it will one day count themselves lucky to have escaped its unforeseen late complications. Those patients who are initially denied possible benefit are also automatically protected from possible harm. Mere hindsight helps nobody.

A Valid Distinction?

Can we get this sort of thing across to our critics? Unfortunately, many professional statements and attitudes add to the difficulties of doing so. Not only the British Medical Association's *Handbook of Medical Ethics*[9] but also *The Dictionary of Medical Ethics*[10] and several reports summarising the work of ethical committees[11,12], make little or no attempt to make this vital distinction between randomised treatment on the one hand and "research" (in the sense in which most people use the word) on the other. Either the writers do not agree that there is an important distinction; or they agree, but despair of ever convincing public opinion (partly because of semantic difficulties) and feel it is safer just to lump everything together under the heading of "clinical research". This gives a misleading impression of what randomised treatment is all about. "Research" and "experiment" are words that have no precise definition; some would use them about randomised treatment, others would not. They cannot be proved inaccurate; but they are certainly misleading. A doctor who contributes to randomised treatment trials should not be thought of as a research worker, but simply as a clinician with an ethical duty to his patients not to go on giving them treatments without doing everything possible to assess their true worth. All who prefer a humble doctor to an arrogant one should note that it is the former who tends to support randomised trials.

Every time we apply the same yardstick to randomised treatment trials that we do to non-therapeutic research, we blur the essential distinction between the two. "The ethical physician," says the Code of Conduct of the Canadian Medical Association[13], "will, before initiating any clinical research, ensure that the individuals are unlikely to suffer any harm." This advice — vital for "research" — is quite inappropriate for randomised treatment, where a decidedly hazardous policy — believed by those who practice it to be justified by its benefits and by the serious consequences of inadequate treatment — might very usefully and ethically be compared with something less hazardous (but quite possibly less effective). Yet, as in the BMA handbook, little or no attempt is made to make this important distinction clear.

Another source of confused thinking arises when it is suggested that randomised treatment is ethically undesirable for certain groups such as the very elderly or the dying. This is surely incorrect. If we really care about all our patients, not just some of them, we want to know as much as possible about the advantages and disadvantages of different ways of trying to help any and all of them. Not just impressions and prejudice, but sound evidence. Randomised treatment (with or without special consent) provides an ethical way of obtaining it. Logistically there are severe constraints, but not ethically. If we insist that randomised treatment requires the same informed consent as "research", then many groups of patients — the unconscious or semiconscious, the seriously disturbed, the mentally defective, and many others who badly need our help — are going to be denied the benefits of randomised comparisons.

Another point is the use of such phrases as "control group" and "end point", as used in laboratory experiments. In randomised treatment trials such terms (erroneously thought to give a scientific gloss to a protocol) are unnecessary, inappropriate, and give the wrong impression. When analysing the results of different treatments, the research worker may well choose to focus only on certain aspects, but the clinician must always study all the advantages and disadvantages to the patient of each policy. Worse still is the sort of statement occasionally still seen in trial protocols — "analgesics may be given as necessary". It makes the flesh creep that anyone should feel the need to say this when treatment policies are being compared. No wonder randomised treatment is confused with "research" if we say things like this.

Finally, randomised treatment, no matter how safe or well established, is usually referred to ethical committees for approval, whereas many non-randomised new or hazardous treatments are not. This is doubtless partly because newness and risk are so difficult to define (how new? how risky?) and because it would become increasingly absurd if every difficult clinical decision (there is ethics in all of them) were examined by a committee. But whatever the reason, a vital distinction is lost sight of; and the misleading idea of randomised treatment as "experimental research" is reinforced.

Pros and Cons

If randomised treatment does not ethically require the special consent so necessary in "research", we need to review the advantages and disadvantages of it to the patient. On the credit side is the fact that some patients thrive on a diet rich in detailed information about their illness;

some like the "status" of giving special consent; others feel reassured by it, even when it is little more than a formality. But against this are a number of serious snags, some of which have already been mentioned. Randomisation is bound to sound strange and wrong to many patients. If there are doctors and lawyers who see it only as "human experimentation", what chance is there of the majority of patients grasping the need for it and the ethics of it? The mere fact,that special written consent is thought to be necessary may give the patient (and his relatives and everyone else) the wrong impression. Secondly, if informed consent is to come anywhere near to being what it is supposed to be, we have to describe not only likely hazards but unlikely ones — and we have to do this not just for one treatment policy but for those in the randomised trial and others not in the trial. Increasing detail often leads to increasing confusion[14] — for example, as to which hazard goes with which treatment. If all this is written down for the patient there may be less risk of certain kinds of misunderstanding, but cold print may still further increase the risk of exaggerated fears. Many patients (including many doctors when they are ill, as described so eloquently by Franz Ingelfinger[15] before he died) have no wish to hear about all the benefits and hazards of different options. They just want to get started with a line of treatment that is fully supported by their doctor — a doctor whom they trust (if they do not, they should choose another), who is sincerely interested in their problems, anxious to help, and ethically totally committed to their care — all of which is fully consistent with giving randomised treatment, with or without special consent.

What about priorities? Time spent on obtaining informed consent, when there is no logical ethical need for it, is time that could have been spent on more important aspects of patient care. And if all patients entering randomised treatment trials are to be given details of each option, then — to be consistent — all patients consulting doctors for any reason must be told about all alternative methods. Where does it all end? Is it to be left to our common sense and judgment, recognising that some patients need a lot of information of this kind, while others prefer to trust the advice they are given — or is it to become a matter of "ethics" and compulsion?

Other disadvantages of informed consent have recently been emphasised[16]. For example, is there not a danger that once in possession of written consent some doctors might become a little less concerned than they should be about their ethical responsibilites? This is one of several ways in which the effect of compulsory written consent could be the opposite of what those who advocate it intend.

Should the patient be asked to choose whether or not he wants full information about such matters as hazard, newness of treatment, and randomisation of treatment? Only the inexperienced or the insensitive advise this sort of direct questioning as a routine. If the patient half-heartedly says "yes" (because he feels it is expected of him and it would be cowardly not to) he may then hear frightening things that he would really prefer not to know about. If he says "no", then he may worry about the need for the question and also whether he should have said "yes". A doctor who really cares for his patients needs to use a little more sense and subtlety than this when he assesses — as best he can — their need for information.

Whatever dilemma we are considering — hazard, newness, randomisation, or consent — there is always one acid test, one crunch question. How would a doctor feel if he or one of his family (preferably one he is especially fond of) were ill and included in a randomised treatment trial (perhaps including new or hazardous treatment) without their knowledge or consent? Well, if I can be forgiven for being personal and specific for a minute, it so happens that a few years ago I had a cholecystectomy for gallstones that had been causing obstructive jaundice. Suppose I discover that my case was included without my consent in a randomised trial to compare two surgical techniques. Would I mind? Why should I? I trusted the surgeon, as I hope my patients trust me. Even if one of the techniques was very new and experimental, the possibility of unforeseen hazards would be compensated for by the hope of a lower complication rate — else why should any sane, responsible surgeon want to try it? As for informed consent, I would be grateful that the surgeon had the sense to see that this was not only unnecessary in my case, but undesirable as well. Why should I want to hear, at this particular moment, of surgical complications that I was previously only dimly aware of? Even the most brilliant statistician, informed on the night before undergoing surgery, of some very small but very unpleasant risk, might well lie awake thinking about it. Which of us can rid our minds of fears merely by telling ourselves that we are being irrational to worry about so small a risk? As a past and future patient, I object to the idea of compulsory informed consent; and I also object to the idea that I should always be asked, when ill, if I want information of this kind or not, since such a question could easily spark off considerable anxiety.

Conclusion

Randomised treatment should be thought of, not as research, but as a useful — some would say essential — way of combining appropriate treatment with treatment assessment. It has important limitations, but it is ethical and in the public interest. Without it, comparisons of different kinds of benefit and hazard are often very unreliable. It is always open to anyone to criticise a trial protocol; or to disagree with the vital decision that is taken each time it is decided that the entry of a particular patient into a particular trial constitutes appropriate management.

But the idea that the mere fact of randomisation always requires special informed consent — with all its disadvantages and potential for causing misconception and anxiety — is surely illogical. A doctor in his normal practice, giving treatment without randomisation, is trusted to choose from several options, even though there may be no way that he can be sure which is best. Why should we not also trust a doctor who submits such options to randomisation, while taking full responsibility for the suitability of each? Are the two situations really so different?

Unfortunately we are saddled with problems caused by the sound of it, the thought of it, the misleading aura of experimentation, making it very difficult to devise any code of conduct that reassures the public and the media, yet spares patients from the various harmful effects outlined.

Meanwhile, there is perhaps no harm in reaffirming the view that the best policy — not perfect, but better than any alternative — is for a responsible caring doctor to be flexible, considerate, and discrete, never imposing unnecessary "informed consent", yet always ready to discuss anything with patients who wish it. Far from being patronising or arrogant, such a policy enhances the dignity of the patient as a unique individual, with changing moods and a changing ability to cope with fear, doubt, and uncertainty. At the end of the day it shows more respect for him, or her, than any measure designed to standardise consent and treat everybody alike. If we are not to be trusted with this task, if informed consent to randomised treatment is to become compulsory, then that's sad because a lot of patients will be worse off — but if it comes, we shall just have to make the best of it and cushion the adverse effects as best we can.

References

1. Leading article. Ethics of human experimentation. *Br Med J* 1963; **ii**: 1–2.

2. Bradford Hill A. Medical ethics and controlled trials. *Br Med J* 1963; **i**: 1043–49.

3. Atkins H. Conduct of a controlled clinical trial. *Br Med J* 1966; **ii**: 377–79

4.   Paterson R, Russell MH. Clinical trials in malignant disease, part 3. Breast cancer: evaluation of postoperative radiotherapy. *J Fac Radiol* 1959; **10**: 175–77.

5.   Brahams D. Death of a patient who was unwitting subject of randomised controlled trial of cancer treatment. *Lancet* 1982; i: 1028-29.

6.   Brewin TB The cancer patient: communication and morale *Br Med J* 1977; **ii**: 1623-27.

7.   Declaration of Helsinki. World Medical Association, 1963. *Br Med J* 1964; **ii**: 177.

8.   Report of the Medical Research Council, 1962–63. Cmnd 2382. London: HM Stationery Office, 1964: 21–25.

9.   The handbook of medical ethics. London: British Medical Association, 1981.

10.   Duncan AS, Dunstan GR, Welbourn RB, eds. The dictionary of medical ethics. London: Darton, Longman and Todd, 1981.

11.   Applications for ethical approval: report by a working group, Northern Regional Health Authority. *Lancet* 1978; i: 87–89.

12.   Allen PA, Waters WE. Development of an ethical committee and its effect on research design. *Lancet* 1982; i: 1233–36.

13.   Code of ethics of the Canadian Medical Association. Reproduced in B. M. A. Handbook of medical ethics. 1981: p76.

14.   Ingelfinger FJ. Informed (but uneducated) consent. *N Engl J Med* 1972; **287**: 465–66.

15.   Ingelfinger FJ. Arrogance. *N Engl J Med* 1980; **303**: 1507–11.

16.   Lewis PJ. The drawbacks of research ethics committees. *J Med Ethics* 1982; **8**: 61–64.

Valid comparison is the key

Reprinted from
Medical ethics and/or ethical medicine,
Eds. Razis DV *et al* 1989, Elsevier, Paris, pages 153–156

Summary

In the history of medicine the treatment given to patients has far too often been based on false comparisons between different options. Often the reason has been selection bias. Of the various ways of minimising this, the randomized trial has fewer fallacies than other methods.

Having minimized selection bias, all the advantages and disadvantages of each policy can be compared. The doctor is then equipped with reasonably reliable information on which to base the decision he makes (or the advice he gives) about each patient.

Provided only suitable patients are entered into a trial each patient is just as safe with randomized treatment as with non-randomized treatment. No extra risk is involved. There is no more sacrifice on behalf of other patients than with non-randomized treatment. But it is difficult to convince the public of this.

Unless we blindly obey authority or so called "standard" treatments, every time we see a patient we have a choice to make and this choice must always depend on options. Very often we do not have as much evidence as we would like. The reliability of the evidence depends on: (1) accurate data, (2) the statistical significance of any comparison, (3) selection — are we comparing like with like? Many doctors feel uncomfortable about randomizing treatment — and many patients distrust it — because of the traditional idea that "the doctor knows what is best" and should prescribe just this. But the honest humble doctor knows that often this is not really so. Provided he makes quite sure that each patient entering into a trial is equally suitable for each of the alternative treatments, the patient is just as safe as he is when non-randomized treatment is given[1,2].

Other methods of dealing with the problem of selection bias can be helpful, but the history of medicine in this century shows clearly that they are not so reliable. Matching and staging is full of fallacies. Different doctors and different centres define their stages differently. For example, borderline cases are frequent and, when this happens, some doctors put the case into the earlier stage, some into the later stage. Those who do the latter will automatically seem to be getting better results than those who do the former. Historical comparisons are also unreliable. Staging may become more sophisticated. Supportive therapy may improve. The natural history of the disease may change (not only may certain kinds of cancer become more common or less common for unknown reasons, they may also become more malignant or less malignant). The whole population may live longer and this may improve the survival of cancer patients as well as others. To call the results of treatment in one kind of cancer "very satisfactory" because of a high survival rate and in another kind of cancer "very unsatisfactory" because of a low survival rate is obviously wrong. There is no evidence at all in a statement of this kind that the first treatment is achieving more than the second. It could be achieving less. It could be that, as a result of treatment, the bad prognosis cancer is not doing as badly as it would without treatment. The good prognosis cancer, on the other hand, might do just as well (as far as survival is concerned) without treatment.

But even if two methods of treating *the same* kind of cancer are compared and one shows a much better survival than the other (and the difference is highly significant statistically) there is still *no reason whatever* to think that the first treatment is preferable to the second unless the problem of selection bias has been dealt with. Every medical student should be taught this and there is no need for it to be taught by a statistician; every doctor should be able to teach it.

It is very easy for those of us treating cancer to imagine that better results are due to a more drastic treatment. Randomized trials comparing drastic treatment with less drastic treatment are vital in order to protect patients from needless risk and the early or late side effects of unnecessarily aggressive treatment. The comparison is ethical because those who are denied possible benefit are also shielded from possible unnecessary harm — and nobody knows which it will turn out to be in the end.

If at first one group seems to be doing better, this certainly does not mean that the trial should be stopped. In cancer therapy there is a distinct possibility that in the end the other group will come out best — partly because the benefit in the first group turns out to be only transient and partly because, following this transient benefit, there may be serious late side effects from the more aggressive treatment.

As long ago as in 1949, the radiotherapy centre at the Christie Hospital, Manchester, England, started a randomized comparison, either giving radiotherapy following mastectomy for breast carcinoma or not giving it. In 1955 a total of 1,461 patients had been entered[3]. This was one of the very first randomized trials of cancer therapy. Having minimised selection bias, it showed clearly that the effect on survival, if any, was very small, but that there was a significant beneficial effect in making local recurrence less likely. Having got two comparable groups, other differences (or possible differences) can also be carefully compared, including early and late morbidity. The traditional question in a "scientific" experiment is 'to ask only one question' and then answer it as precisely as possible. But randomized treatment is purely to get rid of selection bias and allow *all* the advantages and disadvantages of each method to be compared. A strong case can be made out for saying that it is unethical of us if we do *not* do this. If more randomized trials had been done in this century — or done earlier than they were — many patients would have been saved from unnecessarily severe treatment (that was later shown to be achieving much less than had been hoped).

It is natural and inevitable that many randomized trials will show that any difference in survival is doubtful. Unless the numbers in a trial are very large, it is possible only to say that the difference, if any, must be small; but this is very valuable information. Small differences in survival are not important compared with the severity and morbidity of a treatment — which would be justified only if the advantage is large. And, as has been said above, when there is no statistically significant difference in survival, there may be statistically significant differences of other kinds, for example early or late side effects (including psychological effects).

Most of the patients I see do not enter any randomized trial. But this is for logistical reasons, not ethical. In my view, it would be perfectly ethical and very desirable — to carry out far more randomized comparisons than we do. There is also no reason (apart from the problem of logistics) why many patients should not be simultaneously in several trials, perhaps one to compare their main treatment (for example, surgery or radiotherapy) and another to compare the tablets they get to help them to sleep and so on.

It is usually best to have treatment in the two arms of the trial differing in only *one way*. This allows a conclusion as to *why* the advantages and disadvantages of two methods showed a significant difference. This can lead to improving treatment more quickly than if we merely do a comparison between two policies which vary in several different ways. Nevertheless, the latter comparison can be very useful, since — until randomization is done — both policies may be in use by reputable doctors but nobody fully understands the pros and cons of each, nobody knows "which is best".

There is no ethical reason why pilot trials should not be randomized. The newer the treatment, the more desirable it is that instead of giving it to all suitable patients, a randomized comparison should be made. In that way, at least some of the patients will be protected from possible harm from the relatively untested treatment. The difficult decision, if it is relatively untested, is whether to give it or not. If it is correct to give it, it is correct also to have a comparable series where the treatment is not given.

The problem of consent

Every patient has a right to full information about his treatment — whether randomized or not randomized — but we all know that full information and full understanding are not possible. Unless we can persuade the public otherwise, we have to inform them each time a treatment is randomized. Logically, the amount of information they need about risks and alternatives is no greater than when non-randomized treatment is given. But so long as the public (and many doctors) believe that the mere act of randomizing treatment constitutes "research" rather than "treatment" — and so long as they think that the patient is now getting treatment that he would not otherwise get — we have no choice but to go along with this.

The problem is always *how much* explanation, and *how much* participation in decision making. One disadvantage of trying to explain randomization (especially if written permission is obtained), is that the patient gets a wrong impression. They think that this is now "research" rather than "treatment".

The vital question is: is the patient making any sacrifice, or being exposed to any increased risk, in the interests of research[4-6]? If so, a full explanation is vital. There can be no question about that. But, if everything is being done purely for his benefit, with no good evidence that any other policy be preferable then — as with non-randomized treatment — a sensitive compassionate doctor will vary the amount of information according to how frightened the patient is, how much paternalism he needs, and how likely he is to understand what is said. The advantages and disadvantages for each patient can then be assessed. What is done now is not "ethical" or "unethical", but sensible and compassionate or not so sensible and not so compassionate.

Under these circumstances, the *advantages* to the patient of having plenty of information include: (1) it gives him a feeling of "autonomy", (2) it may protect him from bad advice or unethical treatment, (3) only he knows his own priorities — though a good doctor will always take these into consideration, and (4) for some patients — but not all — knowledge is an antidote to fear and with plenty of knowledge they feel less frightened.

The *disadvantages* are seldom mentioned these days, but are just as important for every good doctor to bear in mind as are the advantages. These disadvantages include: (1) the risk of creating increased fear and anxiety — a good doctor prefers his patient to be less frightened after he has seen him, not more frightened; (2) the risk of misconception as to what is being done — a danger that is constantly underestimated by experts on law and ethics (who seem to think only of the problem as to whether or not the patient "should be told the full truth"); (3) it may have a harmful effect on the feeling of security, which many ill and frightened patients badly need, if their suffering is to be reduced rather than increased; (4) there is at least some possibility that written consent may make a doctor a little less careful than he should be about what he does, since he may feel that the written consent absolves him from any further anxieties on the subject.

One possible compromise is probably unacceptable at present, but one day — when both the medical profession and the public have a better understanding of the ethics and the problems concerned — might be worth thinking about. The patient entering hospital would sign some form such as this (of course, the exact wording is not easy and would have to be discussed very carefully):

"I freely agree to be treated by this medical team, who frequently randomize treatments of various kinds in order to make accurate comparisons of disadvantages and advantages. I trust the doctors concerned:(1) to ask me if they want me to volunteer for anything involving a sacrifice on my behalf, so that other patients may benefit, and (2) when randomizing treatment without consultation with me, never to give me any treatment that is not appropriate; and that is not just as much in my best interests as it would be if no randomizing was being done. I appreciate that by not asking for full details I am saving the doctors and nurses a lot of valuable time, which they can give to more important aspects of patient care."

References

1. Silverman W.A. (1985) *Human Experimentation.* Oxford University Press, Oxford, U.K.

2. Chalmers I. (1983) Scientific enquiry and authoritarianism in perinatal care and education. *Birth,* **10**: 151–164.

3. Paterson R. & Russell M.H. (1959) Clinical trials in malignant disease. Breast cancer: evaluation in post-operative radiotherapy. *J. Fac. Radiol.,* **10**: 175.

4. Bradford Hill A. (1963) Medical ethics and controlled trials. *Br. Med. J,* **1**: 1043.

5. Atkins H. (1966) Conduct of a controlled clinical trial. *Br. Med. J.,* **2**: 377.

6. Brewin T.B. (1982) Consent to randomized treatment. *Lancet,* **ii**: 919.

I am reminded of another surgeon writing about breast cancer 20 years ago who spoke on one page (if I exaggerate I do so only very slightly, I promise you) of the remarkable and heartening response of 50% of advanced cases to adrenalectomy (his operation) and on the next page of how he could not recommend hypophysectomy (a treatment he was unable to perform himself) because it completely failed in half the cases in which it was tried.

(Extract from a letter to the Editor, *Brit Med J* 1970 i 1050)

SIR —

If a new treatment for recurrent glioma, however ingenious, is followed by a median survival of only 31 weeks, compared with 23 weeks in controls, should this really be described as 'an effective treatment' in the way that Brem and colleagues (April 22, p 1008) do in their abstract? Having told us that those treated in this way live a few weeks longer than untreated controls, why do they not just leave it at that? Readers can then decide for themselves whether to call this an effective treatment — or a treatment that is having very little effect.

(Letter to the Editor, *The Lancet* 1995 **345** 1571)